DATE DUE

Behind Barbed Wire

The Story of Japanese-American Internment during World War II

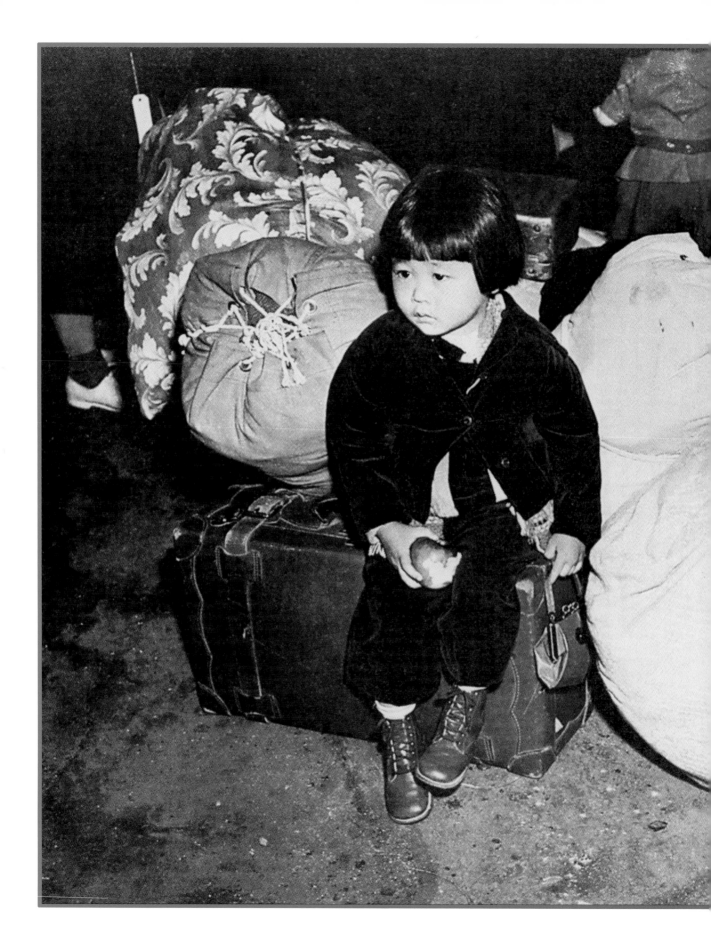

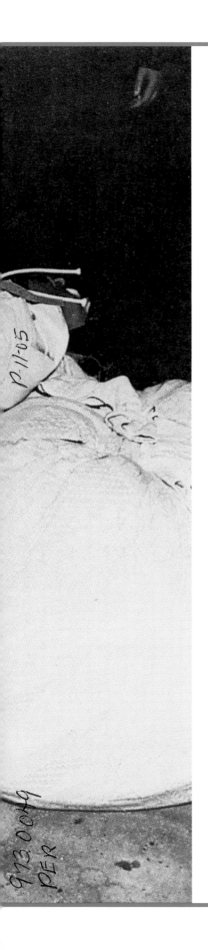

GREAT JOURNEYS

Behind Barbed Wire

The Story of Japanese-American Internment during World War II

by Lila Perl

BENCHMARK BOOKS

MARSHALL CAVENDISH
NEW YORK

Benchmark Books
Marshall Cavendish
99 White Plains Road
Tarrytown, NY 10591-9001

© 2003 by Lila Perl
Maps copyright © 2003 by Marshall Cavendish Corporation
Maps by Rodica Prato

Cover photograph: *Wearing identification tags, members of a Japanese-American family await
transport to the internment camp.*

Photo Research by Candlepants Incorporated
Cover Photo: Dorothea Lange/WRA National Archives
The photographs in this book are used by permission and through the courtesy of:
National Archives: 46, 51, 69, 94. Dorothea Lange, WRA: 2–3, 32, 37, 53, 76.
Clem Albers, WRA: 40; Ansel Adams, 54, 63, 64, 65, 67, 68, 70, 96. Photographer
Unknown, WRA: 71, 84, 87, 98. Francis Stewart, 86. *Corbis*: 8, 38, 45, 49, 60, 72.
Horace Bristol, 18. Bettmann: 25, 34, 83. Wally McNamee, 92 (top). Dean Wong, 102.
Michael Yamashita: 106. *Gift of Madeleine Sugimoto and Naomi Tagawa, Japanese American
National Museum*: 10. Bishop Museum: 14 (left), 28. C. Furneaux: 20. *Hawaii State
Archives*: 14–15. *Courtesy of the Department of Special Collections, University Research Library,
UCLA*: 22. *U.S. Army Photo*: 88, 92 (bottom). *Wide World Photo*: 100.

Library of Congress Cataloging-in-Publication Data
Perl, Lila
Behind barbed wire: the story of Japanese-American internment during
World War II/ by Lila Perl.
p. cm — (Great journeys)
Includes bibliography and index.
Summary: Discusses the forced internment of Japanese Americans in camps following the
attack on Pearl Harbor and the entry of the United States into World War II.
ISBN 0-7614-1321-9
1. Japanese Americans—Evacuation and relocation, 1942–1945—Juvenile literature.
2. World War, 1939–1945—Prisoners and prisons, American—Juvenile literature.
3. World War, 1939–1945—Concentration camps—United States—Juvenile literature.
[1. Japanese Americans—Evacuation and relocation, 1942–1945. 2. World War,
1939–1945—Concentration camps—United States. 3. World War, 1939–1945—Japanese
Americans. 4. World War, 1939–1945—United States.] I. Title. II. Great Journeys
(Benchmark Books (Firm))

D769.8.A6 P47   2002   973'.004956--dc21   2001043337

Printed in the United States of America

1 3 5 6 4 2

Contents

Also by Lila Perl

North Across the Border: The Story of the Mexican Americans

Four Perfect Pebbles: A Holocaust Story (with Marion Blumenthal Lazan)

Guatemala: Central America's Living Past

It Happened in America: True Stories from the Fifty States

Mexico: Crucible of the Americas

Mummies, Tombs, and Treasure: Secrets of Ancient Egypt

Piñatas and Paper Flowers/Piñatas y Flores de Papel

Puerto Rico: Island between Two Worlds

Slumps, Grunts, and Snickerdoodles: What Colonial America Ate and Why

The Great Ancestor Hunt: The Fun of Finding out Who You Are

Foreword

EARLY ON THE MORNING OF SUNDAY, DECEMBER 7, 1941, MORE THAN 360 Japanese warplanes roared out of the sky over the United States naval base on the Hawaiian island of Oahu. Within less than two hours, the surprise assault on the American fleet anchored at Pearl Harbor had resulted in the destruction of 21 ships (including 7 battleships), and more than 300 army and navy planes.

The attack, that quiet Sunday morning, on the U.S. possession known as the Territory of Hawaii, also caused a large number of casualties. Nearly 2,400 persons, most of them military personnel, were killed, and about 2,000 were injured.

In 1941, the United States was not yet officially involved in World War II. Ever since the war had broken out in Europe in September 1939, there had been a debate between those who were against U.S. involvement

The attack on Pearl Harbor led to the United States's involvement in World War II—and the imprisonment of 120,000 Japanese people living in this country.

and those who wanted the country to join in the fighting.

By early 1941, however, the nation's position shifted from neutrality (not taking sides) to preparedness. America had begun to expand its armed forces, build defense plants, and provide war materials to Great Britain and France. Those countries were known as the Allied forces.

Germany, Italy, and Japan, known as the Axis nations, were locked in the struggle with the Allies. Japan's sneak attack on Pearl Harbor, which had been carefully conceived and executed, swiftly decided the question of America's active participation in the war.

December 7, the date of the attack on Pearl Harbor, was denounced by President Franklin Delano Roosevelt as "a date which will live in infamy." The following day the United States declared war on Japan and, a few days later, on its European Axis partners.

A detailed accounting of the devastation inflicted at Pearl Harbor had hardly begun when a wave of hysteria directed at the U.S.'s Japanese-American population began to sweep the nation. It was fueled by the suspicion that the Japanese residents of both Hawaii and the mainland had somehow aided and abetted the Pearl Harbor attack by acting as spies and saboteurs.

Within days the public, the news media, and local officials on the West Coast of the U.S. began to call for the removal and incarceration of all Japanese residing in their communities. In February 1942, this demand resulted in a presidential order that led to the imprisonment on American soil of 120,000 men, women, and children of Japanese ancestry, two-thirds of whom were American citizens.

Without a single case of a Japanese American having committed a treasonous act, the Japanese-American residents of the states of California, Oregon, and Washington had to sell or otherwise dispose of their possessions on short notice and report to temporary assembly centers. They were then moved to permanent internment camps.

The camps were located in isolated regions, mainly desert areas of the interior West. They were fenced with barbed wire and patrolled by armed guards. Families were housed in hastily built barracks of wood and tar paper. Living conditions were crude, and only the most basic necessities were provided.

In these raw and dreary surroundings, the Japanese from America's West Coast lived out the war. They lost their homes and property, their savings, their health, their family structure, their human dignity, and, above all, their personal freedom.

February 19, 1942, the date on which President Franklin D. Roosevelt signed the executive order that imposed the segregation and incarceration of Japanese Americans, may well be regarded as another "date of infamy" in American history.

男児志を立て郷関を出づ
学業若し成らずんば死すとも帰らず
骨を埋むる豈唯墳墓の地のみならんや
人間到る処に青山あり

Symbols such as a rice bag and a glowing lantern were thought to bring good fortune to Japanese people who were about to travel far from home.

One

Dreams of Fortune

Huge dreams of fortune
Go with me to foreign lands,
Across the ocean.

THESE LINES GIVE VOICE TO THE ASPIRATIONS OF THE FIRST JAPANESE PEOPLE
to leave their homeland and to voyage across the Pacific. Their emigration
started in the latter half of the 1800s.

For more than two hundred years, beginning in 1639, the inhabitants
of Japan were forbidden to travel abroad. This was the period of the
shogunate, or military dictatorship, of the Tokugawa family. In this period,
foreign influences were seen as a threat to national security. The arrival in
1853 of the American naval officer Commodore Matthew C. Perry and

his squadron of four ships started a gradual change in Japan's isolationist attitude toward the West.

It was not, however, until the overthrow of the Tokugawa shogunate, in 1867, and the restoration of a single imperial ruler, Emperor Mutsuhito, in 1868, that the ban on emigration began to be lifted. Mutsuhito called himself the Meiji (enlightened rule) emperor.

That year 148 Japanese laborers were recruited to work on sugar plantations in the Kingdom of Hawaii. Their emigration was arranged through negotiations between the Hawaiian consul general and the Japanese government. Although around 40 laborers returned to Japan pleading mistreatment, the emigration of Japanese workers had begun.

In 1869, according to reports, an enterprising German merchant, John Henry Schnell, brought about 35 Japanese to California for silk farming and tea growing. Schnell's enterprise soon failed, for the California climate, at a place called Gold Hill, near Sacramento, was not suited to the cultivation of mulberries for silkworm production or the growing of tea. Schnell's group disbanded and its Japanese members were most likely absorbed into the local Asian population, which was at that time mainly Chinese.

During this period, the government of Japan was embarking on a broad and costly program of modernization. The trade agreements negotiated with Commodore Perry convinced the Meiji ruler of the importance of adopting the powerful economies and military strengths of the nations of the West. For Japan to finance its westernization would require a great deal of money. For the bulk of these funds, it turned to the broad base of its economy—farmers.

Throughout the nation's history, Japan's farmers had been taxed a percentage of the value of their crops. But starting in 1873, the government instituted an annual tax on the land its farmers owned. That year also saw the passage of a national conscription law, making military service for young men compulsory. Both of these measures became strong incentives for emigration.

By the 1880s, more than 360,000 Japanese farmers were facing such severe economic hardship that they were forced to sell their lands below market prices to pay their debts. Some lost their lands entirely. The farmers began to starve, subsisting on vegetation, such as leaves and grass, which filled their bellies but had little nutritional value.

In Hawaii, meanwhile, the sugar industry was expanding as a result of an 1875 treaty that permitted the growers to sell their sugar to the United States without having to pay import taxes. Field hands were desperately needed. By 1885, emigration fever had taken hold in Japan—28,000 Japanese had reached Hawaii's shores.

During the next fifteen years, about 65,000 Japanese, most of them destitute farmers, migrated to Hawaii. Most were signed up through government contracts that provided for a five-year stay and a salary of ten dollars a month, plus transportation and lodging. The wage received by a Japanese sugar plantation worker was at least six times that of a day laborer in his native land.

At first, the emigrants did not think of themselves as leaving home permanently, but rather as *dekaseginin*, or temporary laborers. They planned to work in the Hawaiian sugarcane fields only long enough to earn the money required to pay off the family debts and possibly even buy back their lands. Most did send money home, but many did not return.

A typical experience was that of Asakichi Inouye, the grandfather of the U.S. senator from Hawaii, Daniel K. Inouye. Having lost its property because of a fire that damaged nearby houses as well, the Inouye family sent its eldest son, Asakichi, to Hawaii with his wife and small son. Asakichi intended to remain only until he could save enough to repay the losses caused by the fire and restore his family's honor. Although Asakichi sent home all he could, he saw little hope of earning enough money in the cane fields. He decided to remain in Hawaii because he saw more chances to increase his income there.

Hawaii also offered advantages for young men who were subject to

Japanese laborers about to emigrate to Hawaii in the late 1800s were tagged with numbers for the journey.

Sugarcane workers from Japan who were entering Honolulu were first quarantined on an offshore island that was reached by a pedestrian bridge.

the Japanese military draft. If a man stayed away from home until the age of thirty-two, he could no longer be drafted. Also, if a firstborn son left Japan and did not return, a second son who became head of the household became exempt from the draft.

THE 1890s ALSO SAW THE BEGINNINGS OF JAPANESE EMIGRATION TO THE United States mainland. The main lure, as in Hawaii, was higher wages. The mainland was even more appealing, for there one could earn as much as a dollar a day. In Hawaii, one could only earn one-third of that and, in Japan, one-sixth.

Most Japanese immigrants were better educated than America's European immigrants at that time, or than the Chinese who had preceded them to the U.S. mainland some fifty years earlier.

Japan had a system of compulsory education, and many of its inhabitants had at least eight years of schooling. The 1910 U.S. Census revealed that among Japanese immigrants only 9.2 percent were unable to read and write, while among European immigrants 12.7 percent were illiterate.

In Japan, permission to emigrate had to be obtained from the government. The Meiji emperor set up review boards to make sure that those planning to work abroad were healthy and of good moral character, so that no matter where they eventually settled they would uphold Japan's national honor.

The example of the Chinese in America was stressed as a "lesson" in what Japanese immigrants should *not* do. Hardworking but largely illiterate and unprotected by their government, the immigrant Chinese had earned a reputation for drinking, gambling, and other vices. They had also been condemned for competing unfairly with Caucasians because they were willing to work for lower wages. In 1882, Chinese laborers were banned from further immigration into the United States through the passage of the Chinese Exclusion Act.

On February 13, 1884, the Japanese consul, Takahashi Shinkichi, told his country's foreign ministry: "It is indeed the ignominious conduct and behavior of indigent Chinese of inferior character . . . that brought upon the Chinese as a whole the contempt of the Westerners and resulted in the enactment of legislation to exclude them from the country."

While most Japanese emigrants to the United States were young men in their twenties, the Japanese government also encouraged young women to go abroad, wisely promoting the development of family life in the new Asian communities of the Pacific Coast of America. Almost from the start, the ratio of women to men was higher than it had been among the Chinese immigrants, and it continued to increase.

Many Japanese who have written of their departure from home tell of their last view of Mount Fuji from Yokohama Harbor. They describe life in the steerage quarters below decks in the rear of the ship, the lack of washing and sanitary facilities, the bad food, the seasickness, the tiring days and nights of the crossing, and the fear of what might await them on their arrival.

The foul odors of engine oil, machinery, smelly cargo, and unwashed human bodies combined with the pitching and rolling of a sea-tossed vessel left passengers little appetite for the monotonous diet of bean-paste soup and pickled radish. But worst of all were thoughts of the home that they might never see again.

"My parents came to see me off at Kobe station," one young woman wrote. "They did not join the crowd, but quietly stood in front of the wall. They didn't say 'good luck,' or 'take care,' or anything. They did not say one word of encouragement to me. They couldn't say anything because they knew, as I did, that I would never return."

"PHOTO MARRIAGE" WAS THE NAME GIVEN TO LONG-DISTANCE MARITAL arrangements in Japan. The families made the selections and the bride and groom exchanged photographs before meeting.

After Japanese men who had gone to America began to want wives,

Mount Fuji was often the last view of Japan that emigrants saw before sailing to America from Yokohama Harbor.

this system was applied in making overseas matches. Japanese women who expressed a desire to emigrate to the United States were soon flooded with proposals, usually through relatives and friends who knew of bachelors living abroad. Sometimes a year or two passed between betrothal and the actual arrival of the "picture bride." But the commitments were firm and resulted in many marriages.

In Japan, 60 percent of women were already in the work force in 1900. Unlike Chinese women, their labor was not restricted to household and farm work. They were engaged in tea processing, papermaking, and the textile industry. They served as barmaids, waitresses, and chambermaids in Japanese inns. They even worked as construction laborers and as coal carriers in the mines.

Many jobs in Japan took women away from their homes. *Dekasegi rodo* was the name for this form of migratory labor. The temporary or even long-term employment of both men and women sprang from the Meiji policy of industrialization.

As with the men, Japanese women were taught to read and write. As early as 1876, English had become a major subject in Japanese schools beyond the elementary grades. By the turn of the century, even women who had not gone beyond elementary school had heard about America, and many wanted to emigrate.

The Hawaiian government had also encouraged Japanese women to emigrate along with men. The women worked on the sugar plantations and also as cooks, seamstresses, and at other skilled employment. After Hawaii became a U.S. territory, in 1900, planters stressed the need for married couples to come to live and work on the islands.

For the picture brides who ventured so far from home, there were bound to be disappointments. On reaching San Francisco, a bride had her first meeting with the man she had contracted to marry. Often a prospective husband bore little resemblance to his photograph. It was not unusual for a laborer to have his picture taken in rented clothing, or for

Hawaii encouraged women, such as this Japanese mother, pictured here sitting with her child, to emigrate with their husbands.

a much older man to have his graying hair and wrinkled face retouched by the photographer to convey a younger appearance.

Almost always, however, the bride went through with the marriage, no matter how disappointed she was. An attempt to return home would shame her parents and those who had volunteered to make the match. In extreme cases, a disillusioned bride might try to make her own way in the new world. All too often, however, such efforts at independence resulted in women being forced into a life of prostitution.

Years after a marriage had taken place and a family had been established, a Japanese picture bride might confess that she had been more eager to get to America than to marry. Michiko Tanaka told her adult daughter: "I had consented to marriage with Papa because I had the dream of seeing America . . . and Papa was a way to get there."

The first Japanese people to arrive in the United States found jobs in lumbering and railroad building on the Pacific Coast.

Two

From a Different Shore

ON ARRIVING IN THE UNITED STATES IN THE 1890s AND EARLY 1900s, Japanese men quickly found jobs in railroad building, mining, construction, and agriculture. They were hired to replace Chinese laborers whose numbers were dwindling as a result of the Chinese Exclusion Act of 1882. But this trend did not continue for long.

Most Japanese immigrants came from families with a long history of farming small independently owned plots. Those who could not afford to buy land outright in the U.S. obtained it through share or leasing arrangements. As male immigrants married and began to raise families, all family members worked very hard to make the small farms productive.

The Japanese had come to America at a time when the country was industrializing rapidly and its cities were growing. Newly developed refrigerator cars could speed perishable produce by rail to distant markets. This development was highly favorable to the Japanese farmers, who specialized in short-term crops and truck vegetables (grown for local markets) such as lettuce, celery, onions, and tomatoes. And, as early as 1910, Japanese farmers were producing 70 percent of California's strawberries.

Many picture brides later recalled the early days of farming alongside their husbands. One young wife described her California farmhouse as a "shack . . . one room, barren, with one wooden bed and a cook-stove—nothing else. The wind blew in . . . through the cracks in the board walls."

Farm work meant rising before dawn, picking and sorting tomatoes for shipment, fixing breakfast for a growing family, then returning to the stooped-over labor required to tend the rows of berries, snap beans, or onions, and often working until dusk.

Yoshiko Ueda remembered, "I was tired out and limp as a rag. . . . Coming back from the fields, the first thing I had to do was start the fire [to cook dinner]. . . . I got down to eighty-five pounds, though my normal weight had been 150."

As the Japanese farming population grew, so did a Japanese presence in the cities of the West Coast. Frequently the very first experience of a Japanese immigrant arriving in San Francisco was exposure to a racial slur. White Americans were all too ready to link the new arrivals with the Chinese, whom they pelted with racial epithets. Passersby called the Japanese "Chinks" and "ching ching Chinamen." They assumed that Japanese and Chinese spoke the same language and that all Asians ate "chop suey."

Once white Americans recognized that the Japanese were a separate racial group, they treated them no better than before. Like the Chinese, the Japanese had come from a different shore, a strange and alien place. As objects of racial hostility, they were "dirty Japs" or "yellow Japs." Sidewalk graffiti said JAPS GO HOME, and signs on highways outside small towns read, NO MORE JAPS WANTED HERE. Spitting and throwing rocks at Japanese immigrants were commonplace. Even when a Caucasian and a Japanese person reached a state of cordiality, the Caucasian often addressed his acquaintance as "Mr. Jap."

By the early 1900s, the success of the Japanese farmers had already made them targets of racism.

Discrimination made it necessary for the Issei (first-generation or Japanese-born) immigrants to form their own small businesses and ethnic communities in the cities. A white barbershop would not cut "animal's hair," the term used for the hair of the Japanese. A white store would not sell to the Japanese, a white restaurant would not serve them, a white boardinghouse would not rent them rooms. So, very quickly, in cities and towns stretching all the way from Los Angeles to Seattle, the Issei developed their own hotels, eateries, barbershops, food and supply stores, tailor shops, laundries, and poolrooms.

Japanese in the coastal communities also bought their own boats and became small-scale independent fishermen. Early on in the era of Japanese immigration, white Americans began to take note of the extraordinary farming success of the Issei, especially on lands that did not appear to be very suitable for raising crops and had therefore been sold for very little. As early as 1907, white farmers in California who saw the Japanese as unfair competition began to agitate for a law that would undermine their success. In 1913, they achieved their goal with the passage of the Alien Land Act, which made it illegal for "aliens ineligible for citizenship" to own land.

Japanese immigrants were the targets of the Land Act. The U.S. government's Naturalization Law of 1790 said that only "white" persons could attain American citizenship through the oath-of-allegiance procedure known as *naturalization*. Even though an 1870 statute had given African Americans citizenship, Asians were still governed by the 1790 law.

The Issei farmers, however, found ways of sidestepping the worst effects of the Alien Land Act. Their children, the Nisei, or second-generation Japanese, *were* American citizens because they were born in the United States. Even Nisei offspring who were not yet of age for land ownership could become landowners with their parents as legal guardians. However, stricter land laws passed in 1920 and 1923 forbade the lease or purchase of land on behalf of minors. Other Issei formed ownership corporations or put their land titles in the names of white friends or business partners. Several western states also passed land acts to restrict Japanese farmers. Some of these laws remained in effect until 1948.

Labor organizations, newspapers, and magazines freely expressed anti-Japanese feeling. On March 17, 1900, the editor of the newspaper *Organized Labor* wrote: "Chinatown with its reeking filth and dirt, its gambling dens and obscene slave pens, its coolie labor and bloodthirsty tongs [secret societies], is a menace to the community; but the snivelling Japanese, who swarms along the streets and cringingly offers his paltry service for a suit of clothes and a front seat in our public schools, is a far greater danger to the laboring portion of society than all the opium-soaked pigtails who have ever blotted the fair name of this beautiful city."

The city referred to was the home of the *San Francisco Chronicle*, which in 1905 published a series labeling the Japanese the "yellow peril," a term that had first been applied to the Chinese. Even though Japanese farmers owned less than 2 percent of California's farmland at the time, they were tagged "land grabbers." One of the *Chronicle*'s racist headlines read: "The Yellow Peril: How Japanese Crowd Out the White Race."

Racial purity was a concern of the organization known as the Native Sons of the Golden West. "Would you like your daughter to marry a Japanese?" the Native Sons asked in their publication, *The Grizzly Bear*. "If not, demand that your representatives in the legislature vote for segregation of whites and Asiatics in the public schools."

In October 1906, the San Francisco school board decreed that henceforth school principals must send "all Chinese, Japanese, and Korean children to the Oriental School." At the time, there were only ninety-three Japanese students attending the San Francisco public schools.

This order, even though it came from a local institution, prompted a sharp protest from the government of Japan, which had maintained a nationalistic concern for its citizens living abroad and for their offspring.

Japan had grown considerably as a military power, especially since the 1905 victory of Admiral Togo over the Russian fleet in the Russo-Japanese War. Japan was also a valuable trading partner, and President Theodore Roosevelt was anxious to avoid an unpleasant confrontation with that nation. Speaking to Congress on December 3, 1906, the president lamented that ". . . a most unworthy feeling has manifested itself against the Japanese . . . shutting them out from the common schools of San Francisco." He denounced the action as "a wicked absurdity," and asked for "fair treatment for the Japanese," as he would for any European immigrant group.

Unlike the United States, in 1907 the Kingdom of Hawaii had such a large Japanese population that there were enough students for an all-Japanese school.

The school controversy resulted in an alteration of the segregation order. Only Chinese and Korean children were barred from the San Francisco public schools. Japanese children could attend. But to pacify the racist elements in the American West, President Roosevelt negotiated the 1907–1908 Gentlemen's Agreement with Japan. No legal documents were signed. The United States and Japan were bound to the terms only by their honor.

The agreement called for Japan to stop issuing passports to laborers who wanted to emigrate to the United States. While it reduced the flow of men entering the country, it did not stop picture brides, wives, children, and even parents of Japanese immigrants from joining them.

Clearly, the anti-Japanese factions in the U.S. were not satisfied with the results of the Gentlemen's Agreement. The size of the Japanese population continued to grow and so did openly discriminatory practices and episodes of violence. The Ladies' Agreement of 1921 terminated the immigration of picture brides. Their number by that time had reached about 20,000, and women made up 35 percent of the Japanese population on the U.S. mainland. But even this measure did not satisfy the demands of the exclusionists.

At last, those who wanted to stop the entry of Japanese nationals achieved their goal. The U.S. Congress passed the Immigration Act of 1924. It forbade the entry of all aliens who were ineligible for citizenship. The act came to be known informally as the Japanese Exclusion Act.

Valentine S. McClatchy, a wealthy California newspaper owner, testified to Congress shortly before the act's passage that: "Of all races ineligible to [sic] citizenship, the Japanese are the least assimilable and the most dangerous to the country. . . . They come . . . for the purpose of colonizing and establishing here the proud Yamato race. They never cease to be Japanese."

From McClatchy's words one might have expected that by 1924 the Japanese had taken over the state of California. Actually, the state's Japanese residents made up only slightly more than 2 percent of its total population.

FOLLOWING THE PASSAGE OF THE 1924 IMMIGRATION ACT, THE JAPANESE in America felt, more than ever, the stigma of being strangers from a different shore.

The Issei, dismayed that no more of their countrymen would be arriving to join them, bonded even more firmly with their peers in the struggle to survive white scorn and hostility.

"The Japanese cannot say they are not clannish," one Issei admitted. "But if they have become more so . . . it is because of restraint, economic deprivation, social ostracism, and political discrimination." While a European could become an "American," another Issei reflected, a Japanese would always be a Japanese because of his all-too-recognizable physical appearance.

An even greater concern for the Issei was the fate of their American-born children, the Nisei. Although they were American citizens, they too were destined to be marked as "different." The Issei worked hard to send their sons and daughters to college so that they might surpass the economic and social status of their parents.

Between 1890 and 1910, the Japanese population of the U.S. mainland increased from only 2,039 to slightly more than 72,000. It consisted mainly of men in their twenties and thirties. By 1930, the Japanese population had nearly doubled, reaching almost 139,000. By this time, many marriages had taken place and enough children had been born so that there were as many Nisei as there were Issei.

The Nisei, like most children of immigrants, had a dual culture. They spoke English fluently but usually knew only a little Japanese, which they spoke at home with their parents. They ate both Japanese and American food, often showing a preference for the latter. They celebrated both Christmas and the Japanese holidays still observed by their parents, such as the emperor's birthday. Often they took American first names as well.

While most Issei parents agreed that both they and their Nisei children had become so separated culturally from Japan that there was no possibility of going there to live, some Issei did choose to send their American-born offspring to Japan for all or part of their education. These young people were known as the Kibei. Some 8,000 of them had three or more years of schooling abroad in the prewar years.

But most seemed to have derived little or no benefit from the experience. The native Japanese found them too foreign, even badly behaved.

On their return to the U.S., Japanese Americans saw them as snobbish and too "Japanesy." As a result, many Kibei became even more unsure of their cultural identity.

BY THE 1930S, IT HAD BECOME EVIDENT THAT NEITHER AMERICAN CITIzenship nor a college education would help the Nisei to break down the barrier of racial discrimination. Professional opportunities in academia, business, manufacturing, engineering, even the public sector, were closed to Japanese.

To make matters worse, the nation was suffering through the Great Depression. Disheartened, many well-educated Nisei found themselves working in the same ethnic labor market as their less-educated parents. They operated fruit stands, grocery stores, laundries, and lodging houses. Some became doctors, dentists, or nurses, but they treated Japanese patients exclusively. Whites would not use their services.

Economically and politically the Nisei faced a barrage of anti-Japanese pressure groups that had been gathering strength since their Issei parents had first ventured ashore. V. S. McClatchy led an organization called the California Joint Immigration Committee (formerly known as the Japanese Exclusion League). It was made up of such racist groups as the Native Sons of the Golden West, the American Legion, the California State Grange, and the California Federation of Labor. All of these associations were closed to Japanese membership. Municipal, county, and state officials were not at all sympathetic to the plight of the despised minority.

During the 1930s, the Nisei tried to reach the liberals in the national political parties. Their long-term quest was for legislation supporting equal rights in employment, housing, and civil liberties. A more immediate achievement was the formation of the Japanese American Citizens League (JACL), which took place at a convention of Nisei professionals in Seattle, Washington, in 1930.

The members of the JACL sit for a group portrait. The organization pledged its loyalty to the United States in 1936 and maintained it throughout internment.

One of its leaders, James Sakamoto, expressed the view that "Instead of worrying about anti-Japanese activity or legislation" the role of the second generation was "to inculcate in all its members the true spirit of American patriotism." Elected as president of the JACL at its 1936 convention, Sakamoto called on all Nisei to demonstrate their loyalty to the United States, socially, economically, and politically, never thinking of themselves as dual citizens but only as Americans.

Not all Nisei were ready to adopt the hypernationalistic stance of the JACL (which was open only to American-born Japanese and to a very few Issei who had gained citizenship through serving in World War I). Yet in 1940, not long before America's entry into World War II, the JACL announced its creed, praising the "opportunities and advantages"

America had given its Japanese citizens, and pledging to "defend her against all enemies." The creed was written by Mike Masaru Masaoka, who became the long-term leader of the JACL.

When war with Japan came a year later, however, the superpatriotism of the JACL did little to endear the Nisei to their Caucasian countrymen. The Japanese were still considered strangers from a different shore who were not to be trusted.

One day after the Japanese attack on Pearl Harbor, President Franklin Delano Roosevelt signed the declaration of war on Japan.

Three

The Face of an Enemy

"I DO REMEMBER PEARL HARBOR DAY," MARY TSUKAMOTO RECALLED years after she and her family had been sent away to a Japanese internment camp in distant Arkansas. "It was a December Sunday and we were [in church] getting ready for our Christmas program. But after the service started, my husband ran in. He had been home that day and heard on the radio . . . that Japan attacked Pearl Harbor. I remember how stunned we all were. And suddenly the whole world went dark."

That very evening, the Federal Bureau of Investigation made its first roundup of suspects, some 700 Japanese businesses and community leaders, Japanese-language teachers, and Buddhist priests living on the West Coast of the United States. Almost all of those taken away, without search or arrest warrants, were Issei.

"Within a day or two," Mary Tsukamoto reported, "we heard that the FBI had taken Mr. Tanigawa and Mr. Tsuji. One Issei, Mr. Owasa, committed suicide. The rumors had it that we were supposed to turn in our cameras and our guns, and they were called in. And then there was talk about sending us away."

As the early months of the war rolled by, Mrs. Tsukamoto and her Japanese neighbors, who lived in a small community nine miles from Sacramento, were told that they were not allowed to travel more than five miles from home. At the same time, a curfew was imposed prohibiting any outdoor movement from 8 P.M. to 6 A.M. "At that time," Mrs. Tsukamoto explained, "everything was in Sacramento, like doctors, banks, and grocery stores." But in order even to get permission to go to Sacramento to get a travel permit from the Wartime Civilian Control Administration, one had to violate the five-mile restriction. "It was ridiculous."

All this time, Mrs. Tsukamoto and her neighbors were trying to think of how they could serve the war effort to prove their loyalty. They wrapped Red Cross bandages, bought war bonds, and took first aid classes. But going out at night to attend classes or a JACL meeting was dangerous because of the curfew. While it was imposed on all Japanese, it also applied to immigrants from the enemy nations of Italy and Germany who lived in the vicinity, but only if they were aliens, and it was loosely enforced on them.

By late March 1942, not even four months after Pearl Harbor, the Japanese on the Pacific Coast had been told to register their families and to prepare to report to an improvised assembly center, the first step toward being assigned to a permanent camp where they would remain for the duration of World War II.

On short notice, often just a matter of days, people had to sell their homes, furniture, and appliances; their businesses; their cars; their possessions of a lifetime—for whatever they could get for them. That was sometimes as little as one-tenth of what they were worth. Pets, chickens, and other livestock often had to be given away, while crops that were

Immediately following Pearl Harbor, many older Issei involved in business and community affairs were illegally arrested on suspicion of treason.

As their owners received evacuation orders, many Japanese businesses were forced to close on short notice.

ready to be harvested had to be left to rot or to be picked by others.

Told they were going to "camp," the Tsukamotos and others thought of camping expeditions in the mountains and made sure they brought along boots and warm clothing. The Tsukamotos arrived by train at the Fresno Assembly Center. They were hot, perspiring from dragging their suitcases, and unhappy about what awaited them. "I saw how terrible it looked," Mrs. Tsukamoto recalled, "the dust, no trees—just barracks and a bunch of people . . . peeking out from behind the fence."

The temporary residents at Fresno made the best of the crude latrines and showers and the humiliating lack of privacy. They even prettified the tar-paper barracks with flower gardens, and they cultivated vegetable patches. They set up schoolrooms for the children and held English classes for the older adults. They were still in California, in a climate and landscape that were familiar.

After five months of living in the army-style holding pen that had been built hastily on the Fresno fairground, the Tsukamotos were moved to the Jerome Relocation Center in Arkansas. It was October 1942.

The Jerome camp in Arkansas was a rude shock. Mary Tsukamoto remembered:

After we were there a while, the cold weather arrived, and they didn't have enough wood to heat the rooms. We had to go into the woods to chop wood . . . school, everything, was closed and the young people were told to go out and work. . . . My daughter was five and she cried for a whole week. She was so upset, because she wanted to go home; she wanted to get away from the camp. Adults felt the same way.

I realized that I needed to be angry not just for myself personally, but for what happened to our people. And also for our country because I really believed it wasn't just the Japanese Americans that were betrayed, but America itself.

Young children waited patiently amid suitcases and bundled family possessions for transfer to the internment camps.

HOW DID THE MASSIVE BETRAYAL OF 120,000 GUILTLESS MEN, WOMEN, and children living on American soil take place? What were the steps that brought about their segregation and incarceration in direct violation of the guarantees of the U.S. Constitution?

Following the bombing of Pearl Harbor, the U.S. government's first act was to send Secretary of the Navy Frank Knox to Hawaii. Knox quickly concluded that the sneak attack was contrived by spies and saboteurs (enemy agents) among the Japanese Hawaiian population. He recommended that all Japanese be removed to one of the outer islands for incarceration.

Knox's recommendation soon met with opposition from the military governor of Hawaii, General Delos Emmons. Hawaii had a population of 157,000 Japanese in 1941. How, Emmons demanded, would it be possible to determine the disloyal among them? If all of them had to be moved to the small leper-colony island of Molokai, how was such a relocation operation to be managed, especially in wartime? Ships and other means of transport were scarce, and the operation would be costly. Besides, the Japanese who worked on Oahu were desperately needed as ships' carpenters, transportation workers, and agricultural laborers.

For a time, Washington sided with Frank Knox. But Emmons won out, especially after he suggested that if the United States wanted to remove Oahu's Japanese inhabitants, they should evacuate them from the islands entirely and relocate them to the mainland. In the end, only some 1,500 Japanese Hawaiians were interned, of whom two-thirds were aliens.

In the meantime, attention was focused increasingly on the Japanese population living on the mainland. Only months before Pearl Harbor, in October and November 1941, a report had been drawn up by a Chicago businessman serving as a special representative of the State Department, Curtis B. Munson, regarding the degree of loyalty among Japanese residents on both Hawaii and the mainland. Reporting to President Roosevelt in November, Munson wrote: "For the most part the local

Japanese are loyal to the United States or, at worst, hope that by remaining quiet they can avoid concentration camps or irresponsible mobs. We do not believe that they would be at the least any more disloyal than any other racial group in the United States with whom we went to war."

Weeks later, when the United States joined the Allies, even J. Edgar Hoover, director of the FBI, told the United States attorney general that he saw no reason for a mass evacuation of the Japanese for security reasons. By December 10, Hoover reported that he had "practically all" the suspects he had planned to arrest in custody—367 Japanese in Hawaii, 924 Japanese on the mainland, 857 Germans, and 147 Italians.

Yet, federal and state officials in the western United States continued to press for a mass evacuation of Japanese residents, and their case was strengthened by the convictions of Lieutenant General John L. DeWitt, who headed the army's Western Defense Command.

On January 4, 1942, speaking at his San Francisco headquarters, DeWitt asserted that: "We are at war and this area—eight states—has been designated a theater of operations. . . . I have little confidence that the enemy aliens are law-abiding or loyal in any sense of the word. Some of them yes; many, no. Particularly the Japanese. I have no confidence in their loyalty whatsoever."

DeWitt's condemnation of the Japanese overrode the conclusions of both the Munson report and the FBI that the Japanese were loyal to the U.S. government. In January, the Radio Intelligence Division of the Federal Communications Commission reported that, having monitored all broadcasts for a period of several months, it had no evidence that would justify the mass relocation of Japanese residents on American soil. This report, too, was ignored.

RACISM WAS CLEARLY AT THE ROOT OF THE MAINLAND INCARCERATION OF most of the U.S.'s 127,000 Japanese residents. Unlike Hawaii, which had a predominantly Asian population, the mainland had a tiny Japanese presence, totaling less than one-tenth of one percent of the entire U.S. population. But clustered as they were in communities on the West Coast, the Japanese were a highly visible minority. In addition, they were envied for their economic success and criticized for their Caucasian-imposed clannishness. Above all, they were objects of scorn because they bore the face of an enemy.

Now the other Asians—Filipinos, Koreans, Chinese—had to seek protection from attack because they were sometimes confused with the Japanese. Some Chinese Americans began wearing lapel buttons stating, "I am a Chinese."

On December 22, 1941, two weeks after Pearl Harbor, *Time* magazine ran an article titled, "How to Tell Your Friends from the Japs." Photos accompanying the article gave examples of Chinese and Japanese faces.

"Japanese," *Time* explained in a totally inaccurate and biased fashion, "are likely to be stockier and broader-hipped than short Chinese. . . . The Chinese expression is . . . more placid, kindly, open; the Japanese more positive, dogmatic, arrogant. Japanese are hesitant, nervous in conversation, laugh loudly at the wrong time . . . walk stiffly erect, hard heeled."

Even more hard-hitting was the January 29, 1942, syndicated column by Hearst newspaper writer Henry McLemore in the *San Francisco Examiner*: "I am for immediate removal of every Japanese to a point deep in the interior. I don't mean a nice part of the interior, either. Herd 'em up, pack 'em off and give 'em the inside room in the badlands. Let 'em be pinched, hurt, hungry and dead up against it. . . . Personally I hate the Japanese."

Patriotic organizations and farming interests joined their voices to those who were urging a mass Japanese internment. *The Grizzly Bear*, published monthly by the Native Sons of the Golden West, reminded its readers in January 1942: "We told you so. Had the warnings been heeded . . . had Japan been denied the privilege of using California as a breeding ground for dual citizens [Nisei];--the treacherous Japs probably would not have attacked Pearl Harbor . . . and this country would not today be at war with Japan."

The California Vegetable Grower-Shipper Association was blunt about "wanting to get rid of the Japs for selfish reasons." A representative told a journalist for the *Saturday Evening Post* on May 9, 1942: "We might as well be honest. We do. It's a question of whether the white man lives on the Pacific Coast or the brown man. They came into this valley to work, and they stayed to take over. . . . If all the Japs were removed tomorrow, we'd never miss them . . . because the white farmers can take over and produce everything the Jap grows."

Inevitably the pressures to evacuate the Japanese resulted in a clamor in Congress, with California representatives pressing for a presidential order granting the Western Defense Command under General DeWitt the authority to implement such an action.

President Franklin Roosevelt was willing to sign such an order. In a memorandum written as early as August 10, 1936, he had instructed the chief of naval operations that any Japanese person living on the island of Oahu who "has any connection with their officers or men [of Japanese ships] should be secretly but definitely identified and his or her name placed on a special list of those who would be the first to be placed in a concentration camp in the event of trouble."

Thus, on February 19, 1942, President Roosevelt signed Executive Order 9066. It empowered the army, through the secretary of war, to designate "military areas" from which "any or all persons may be excluded" for "the successful prosecution of the war."

The presidential order did not specify that any one enemy ethnic group be removed from the so-called war zones. But it was clear from the start that the scattered German and Italian populations of the United States were not the target. Even the sizable number of Italian aliens residing in the San Francisco area were not suspected of committing treasonous acts.

Yet the Japanese of the Pacific Coast were. Neither then nor at any

The signing of Executive Order 9066 meant that the majority of America's Japanese residents would be taken by armed guard to an internment site for the duration of the war.

future time would a single Japanese American be charged, tried, or convicted of any act of espionage or sabotage. Yet Executive Order 9066 was aimed at them.

By late March 1942, instructions for Japanese Americans to report to their local evacuation boards were posted all over the West Coast.

Four

The Roundup

INSTRUCTIONS TO ALL PERSONS OF JAPANESE ANCESTRY LIVING IN THE FOLLOWING AREA:

So began each of the more than one hundred Civilian Exclusion Orders that started to appear on posters in public places all over the West Coast in the weeks after the signing of Executive Order 9066.

The humiliating heading in bold letters was followed by smaller print directing heads of families to report to their local evacuation boards, known as Civilian Control Stations, and to prepare to leave their homes within five or six days or sometimes as little as two days.

The evacuees were to bring with them: "bedding and linens (no mattresses) for each member of the family . . . toilet articles . . . extra clothing . . . and essential personal effects . . . no pets of any kind."

The first compulsory evacuation orders were not posted until late March 1942. General DeWitt and a variety of federal and local officials had gone through a period of indecision as to how to implement the evacuation. For a few weeks, starting on March 2, the general had experimented with a "voluntary" evacuation from what he decided were the most sensitive coastal areas, advising the Japanese who lived there to move inland or risk internment.

Many had no money for travel, spoke little or no English, and had no idea of where to try to resettle. Only 4,889 of the 120,000 Japanese Americans slated for internment attempted to find new homes or to lodge with relatives. General DeWitt's poorly thought-out plan caused enormous suffering on the part of the volunteers. Inland communities, backed by their own local officials, made their hostility clear with signs at town and city limits declaring: No Japs Wanted. Armed vigilantes met migrating Japanese at the Nevada state line. Few of the volunteers relocated successfully. Most, having tasted the threat of mob violence, preferred to wait for compulsory internment.

Foreign- and American-born Japanese were to be included in the roundup. By 1942, Issei men were between fifty-five and sixty-five years of age. Their wives, many of whom had been picture brides, were ten or more years younger, for often it had taken the young men a long time to save up for wives. As a result, many of the Nisei second generation, who were American citizens by birth, were teenagers or even younger.

A number of Issei women were pregnant at the time of the roundup and had to have their labor induced before leaving because the assembly centers lacked adequate hospitals. During the years of incarceration, nearly 6,000 children were born in the camps. Each of the ten permanent relocation centers had a hospital meant to serve its 10,000 or so inhabitants. But often, the hospitals were unable to deal with problem cases due to inferior equipment and staffing.

Children who were the products of mixed marriages were considered Japanese, even if they had as little as one-sixteenth Japanese blood. When Father Hugh T. Lavery of the Catholic Maryknoll Center in Los Angeles

As a first step, the Japanese were registered to be sent to an assembly center; later, they would be moved to a relocation center or permanent camp.

inquired which children from the church orphanage would have to be sent to the camps, Colonel Karl R. Bendetsen, evacuation strategist and chief assistant to General DeWitt, replied: "I am determined that if they have one drop of Japanese blood in them they must go to camp." No one except tuberculosis sufferers (whose illness was contagious), and those who were mentally or physically ill in hospitals, was exempt from the evacuation order.

The JACL, its membership made up exclusively of Nisei, was still a young organization in 1942. In keeping with its creed of loyalty to the United States and faith in the workings of American democracy, it urged full cooperation with the evacuation and relocation program. Its leaders believed that any other course of action would invite suspicion of Japanese allegiance and harsher treatment in the camps.

Many Nissei agreed with the JACL position. Most Issei, on the other hand, were not as eager to prove themselves good Americans as were their sons and daughters, As hardworking immigrants, they felt bitter, betrayed, and humiliated. Among the Issei men, there were a number of suicides.

One Issei, known only as "Mr. H.," wrote in his journal: "This action is against American Constitution, a black spot for Democracy, but Army paid no attention. I will purchase war bonds and stamps if my financial resources will permit, but . . . I am Awfully disappointed."

Mr. H., his wife, who was suffering from a stomach disorder, and their two daughters were sent to the Santa Anita Assembly Center, hastily set up on the racetrack of the same name, about twelve miles from Los Angeles. "Moving day," Mr. H. wrote, "was the most lamentable and sorrowful day in all our life on the Pacific Coast—our foundation built by fifty years of hard toil and planning, was swept away by Army's order. It was Awful Nightmare!"

Wearing tags with numbers on them instead of names, their luggage limited to only what they could carry, the Los Angeles evacuees boarded fifty buses for the trip to the racetrack.

On their arrival, they were met with the sight of eight-foot-high barbed-wire fences, watchtowers, searchlights, and soldiers armed with machine guns. "We are prisoners of WAR!!" Mr. H. declared.

After the family members were assigned to their room, a converted horse stable, they "went to the dining room, 3000 capacity and were

Santa Anita, like all the other assembly centers, was fenced with barbed wire and guarded by military sentries.

served Pork and Beans. We went back to our room," Mr. H. wrote in a gloomy summing up, "and finally four of us lay on the bed for the night."

SIXTEEN ASSEMBLY CENTERS HAD BEEN SET UP BY THE WARTIME CIVILIAN Control Administration (WCCA), which had fallen under the direction of the ruthlessly efficient Colonel Karl Bendetsen. Some, like Santa Anita and Tanforan in California, were former racetracks where many families, like Mr. H.'s, were housed in stalls that had been vacated by horses only days earlier. At Tanforan, single people were lodged in a huge dormitory built beneath the grandstand.

The mattresses were sacks that the evacuees filled with straw. Families were separated by thin partitions through which they could hear the misery and squabblings of the family next door.

Other assembly centers, like the one at Fresno, were erected on former fairgrounds. Some, like the Portland Assembly Center in Oregon, had been livestock exhibition pavilions. Minoru Yasui, an internee who was sent there in May 1942, described the dining hall as: "festooned with yellowish, spiral flypaper hung from posts and rafters. Within a short time the paper would be black with flies caught in the sticky mess. There were horseflies, manure flies, big flies, little flies, flies of all kinds. . . . Flies, after all, usually inhabited livestock barns."

The meals served in the communal halls were nutritionally limited, for they consisted mainly of canned goods—hash, beans, frankfurters— and starches such as bread and potatoes. The Japanese missed the rice and fresh fruits and vegetables they had grown for market and for their own tables. Those who remained in the assembly centers for longer periods— and some stays lasted as long as six months—began to grow modest amounts of produce themselves.

Communal living meant standing in line for almost every need and sharing public facilities like showers and toilets. Even worse than the filth and odors, worse than the manure-sprinkled floors of the former

Tanforan Assembly Center, like Santa Anita, was a former racetrack, so many of the evacuees were housed in what had once been horse stalls.

Evacuees had to wait on a mess line for their meals, which were served in a communal dining hall in both the assembly centers and the permanent camps.

horse barns and chicken coops, was the total lack of privacy, especially in the toilets.

A woman in the Merced Assembly Center in California wrote to a Caucasian friend in June 1942, describing the camp's army-style latrine. "It's not very sanitary and has caused a great deal of constipation. . . . The toilets are one big row of seats, that is, one straight board with holes out about a foot apart with no partitions at all and all the toilets flush together . . . about every five minutes. The younger girls couldn't go to them at first until they couldn't stand it any longer. . . ."

Most of the evacuees had little or no cash. Single adults were given $2.50 a month to make incidental purchases at the post exchange on the camp grounds. A married couple received $4, and a child under sixteen $1. Mr. H. wrote in his journal that "the ready cash we carried from Los Angeles is getting low every day," so he took a job as a cook in the camp, which paid him $12 a month. The small salary, however, was not sufficient for his family's needs. "If Peace will be restored in some future," he wrote, "I won't have any money left in my possession: this Problem worries me days and nights, but I don't have any idea for solution."

WHILE THE OVERWHELMING MAJORITY OF MAINLAND JAPANESE, BOTH ISSEI and Nisei, obeyed the evacuation orders, a few decided to openly challenge their constitutionality.

In 1942, Gordon Hirabayashi was a college student in his senior year at the University of Washington. He was also a member of the Society of Friends, better known as the Quakers. The Quakers were one of the few religious groups that opposed the wholesale evacuation of the Japanese. They accused Colonel Bendetsen and those he served of manufacturing the excuse of "military necessity," when their real motives in ridding the Pacific Coast of the Japanese were economic and political.

To provide a test case, Hirabayashi violated the 8 P.M. to 6 A.M. curfew imposed on all Japanese and refused to report to his assembly center. He was arrested, found guilty on both charges in Seattle federal district court, and sentenced to three months in prison on each count, the sentences to run concurrently.

In pursuit of a higher court decision on the issue of constitutionality, Hirabayashi appealed his case, which eventually reached the U.S. Supreme Court. On June 21, 1943, the highest court in the land unanimously upheld the legality of the curfew but refused to rule on the question of whether the evacuation order had been a violation of Hirabayashi's civil rights. The justices simply backed away from the issue, claiming, in the words of Justice William O. Douglas: "We cannot sit in judgment on the military requirements of that hour."

A similar decision was handed down on that same date in the case of Minoru Yasui. But Yasui received much harsher treatment than Hirabayashi because he had visited Japan with his family in the summer of 1926, when he was ten years old, and because he had been working as an attaché at the Japanese consulate in Chicago, Illinois, since March 1940.

The day after Pearl Harbor, Yasui, an attorney, resigned his job at the consulate and subsequently returned to his home state of Oregon to report for active duty as a second lieutenant in the United States Army Reserve. Like most other reservists of Japanese ancestry who showed up for assignment, he was dismissed. In the meantime, Yasui's father, an Issei agriculturalist, had been accused of being loyal to the emperor of Japan and was interned as a suspected spy.

On March 28, 1942, Yasui purposely violated the curfew, and on May 12, 1942, he refused evacuation to the Portland Assembly Center. He was escorted there by military police. In September 1942, he was moved to Minidoka, a permanent relocation center in Idaho.

When Yasui was finally tried in Portland, Oregon, in November 1942, Judge James Alger Fee of the federal district court found him guilty and imposed the maximum sentence of one year in jail and a $5,000 fine. The judge's reasoning was that, while he felt the curfew to be unconstitutional in the case of a U.S. citizen, he considered Yasui to have given up his citizenship because he had worked for the Japanese consulate. Thus, in view of Yasui's status, the curfew was constitutional.

The United States Supreme Court disagreed with Judge Fee. It ruled that the curfew was legal for all U.S. citizens on whom it was imposed, and it disagreed that Yasui had lost his citizenship. As in the case of

Hirabayashi, however, it refused to rule on the constitutionality of the evacuation orders.

Yasui spent nine months in solitary confinement, from November 1942 to August 1943, in a six-by-eight-foot cell in Portland's Multnomah County Jail. For the first six weeks he was denied baths, shaves, hair or nail trims, or exercise. Throughout his jail time, he slept on a gray canvas hammock, read and wrote in the light of a bare ceiling bulb, and was fed a diet of bread, potatoes, and chicory coffee. After his release and the suspension of his fine, Yasui was sent back to Minidoka.

TWO OTHER TEST CASES LED TO SUPREME COURT DECISIONS THAT WERE NOT rendered until December 18, 1944, when the war in the Pacific was still in progress, but the fear of an invasion of the U.S. mainland had long ago been dismissed by even the most apprehensive members of the military.

Fred Korematsu was a high-school graduate from Oakland, California, who—like other young Japanese in the years before Pearl Harbor—had registered for the draft under the Selective Service Act of 1940. Because he suffered from stomach ulcers, Korematsu was classified 4–F, physically unfit for service. He got a job working for the war effort as a shipyard welder until the attack on Pearl Harbor, at which time he was expelled from the Boilermakers' Union because he was Japanese.

Korematsu, who was about to marry a Caucasian woman, felt he had done everything he could to prove his loyalty. To avoid being evacuated, he finally tried changing his identity—he had plastic surgery and adopted a Hispanic surname.

However, he was discovered and arrested by the FBI for having disobeyed orders for removal to an assembly center. In September 1942, Korematsu was tried and found guilty in federal district court in San Francisco. He was given a suspended sentence and put on probation for five years, but he was sent to a relocation center.

When Korematsu's case finally reached the United States Supreme

Court on appeal, the Court returned a split decision of six to three, upholding the constitutionality of the evacuation order. Even though the decision went against Korematsu, it at least showed the Court's willingness to deal with the complaint, something that was not granted to Hirabayashi or Yasui eighteen months earlier. Also, the three dissenting justices aired their views in condemnation of the evacuation. Justice Frank Murphy declared that the government's exclusion orders as applied to the Japanese fell "into the ugly abyss of racism."

The test case that finally brought a glimmering of hope that justice might one day prevail for all evacuees was that of Mitsuye Endo.

Endo was a twenty-two-year-old typist and a civil service employee of the state of California until the attack on Pearl Harbor, at which time she was dismissed because of her Japanese ancestry. She had never been to Japan and did not speak Japanese. She had a brother who had been drafted into the U.S. Army in 1941. She and her parents were evacuated in 1942 to an assembly center near Sacramento and from there to a relocation camp. Mitsuye Endo was a model of a loyal Japanese American, and her case was sent to the Court to decide whether it was legal to keep a loyal citizen in an internment camp.

Endo waited two and a half years for the Supreme Court's verdict. On December 18, 1944, the Court granted that the War Relocation Authority (WRA) might detain other classes of citizens but had no authority to detain those "who are concededly loyal," and Mitsuye Endo was freed.

Her case left so many unanswered questions about the WRA's right to hold *any* presumably loyal Japanese person in the camps that, to avoid embarrassment, the War Department suddenly announced, one day before the Endo decision—on December 17—that all the camps would be scheduled to close by the end of 1945.

The December 1944 announcements, however, came much too late for the 120,000 evacuees who had already endured years of incarceration. For them, the spring 1942 roundup that robbed them of their homes, their freedom, and their dignity was only the beginning of a long ordeal.

As for the cases of Gordon Hirabayashi, Minoru Yasui, and Fred Korematsu, it took more than forty years, until January 1988, for all three to be completely cleared of the charges against them. By that time, Minoru Yasui had been dead for two years.

After stays of several months at the assembly centers, the internees were told to pack their bags for removal to one of the relocation centers.

Five

In Deserts and Swamps

IN 1942, THE TEST CASES BROUGHT BY MINORU YASUI AND OTHERS WERE only just starting to make their long, stumbling way through the courts. Meanwhile, Japanese Americans on the West Coast were beginning to be moved from the assembly centers to the permanent camps known as relocation centers.

"In September 1942," Minoru Yasui wrote, after enduring a hot summer in the Portland Assembly Center, "trains began pulling into the siding where meat packers used to load cattle, hogs, and sheep. The grapevine had it that we were being moved to someplace in the deserts of Idaho . . . into permanent camps for the duration of the war."

After a slow all-day trip, sitting on seats that were hard planks, the evacuees arrived at Minidoka, a newly built internment camp north of Twin Falls, Idaho. Located in a dry, dusty wasteland dotted with occasional clumps of sagebrush and cactus, this was to be their home "for the duration." Yasui wrote, "Many sat on the baggage in the middle of nowhere and wept."

Ten such permanent camps were ordered built, their sites to be selected by June 1942. They were to be run by the WRA, which was a civil agency, but they would be constructed by the army, guarded by military personnel, and equipped with barbed-wire fences, watchtowers, and searchlights, like the assembly centers. The camps were distributed among seven states—California, Arizona, Idaho, Utah, Wyoming, Colorado, and Arkansas—whose governors specified that the sites were to be distant from centers of population and well patrolled for potential escapees.

The first director of the WRA was Milton Eisenhower, the brother of the army general and future president Dwight D. Eisenhower. Appointed in March 1942, Eisenhower hoped that most of the West Coast Japanese could be relocated to temporary shelters and then resettled, rather quickly, into civilian life in nonmilitary areas. By April, he realized that this goal could not be achieved in the brief time allotted. The government's plans called for a mass evacuation and prisonlike living conditions.

"I feel most deeply," Eisenhower wrote on April 1, 1942, "that when this war is over and we consider calmly this unprecedented migration of 120,000 people, we as Americans are going to regret the unavoidable injustices that may have been done." In June 1942, three months after his appointment, Milton Eisenhower, seeing no way to avoid the mass internment that he opposed, resigned as director of the WRA. Dillon S. Myer took over the challenging job of trying to formulate a fair and rational policy for the administration of the internment camps.

THE PRINCIPAL DIFFERENCE BETWEEN THE ASSEMBLY CENTERS AND THE internment camps was that the latter were located in the interiors of the western states or in Arkansas. Their army-built barracks of wood and tar paper were set up in orderly rows. Each barrack was about 20 feet wide

Most of the sites chosen for the permanent camps were located in inland desert regions, far from centers of population.

and 120 feet long. The interiors were then divided into four to six one-room "apartments," each assigned to a family.

The dwellings were unfurnished, except for army cots, a pot-bellied stove that burned wood, coal, or oil, and a bare hanging light bulb. Running water was available only in the laundry rooms, showers, and latrines.

Mary Oda, a medical student in 1942 when she and her family were interned at Manzanar, in a valley near California's eastern Sierras, described their room. It measured only about 20 by 25 feet but contained eight cots, each with a mattress the evacuees stuffed with straw, as in the assembly centers.

"We shared the room with an elderly couple in their eighties, a Christian minister and his wife. The room had no inner wall, [just] studs exposing two-by-fours. . . . The floor was wooden, with half-inch gaps

The Manzanar Relocation Center was in a dry valley in California's eastern Sierras.

between the planks where you could see the earth below and through which the winds blew up layers of sand and dust everywhere."

Sand and dust plagued the internees in most of the camps that had been built in desert regions. Manzanar, which means "apple orchard" in Spanish, was in what had once been a fertile valley. Now it had become a manmade desert. The government had bought all the farms in the early 1900s, and then diverted the waters that fed the valley in order to serve the growing city of Los Angeles.

Topaz, in Utah, was a true desert. Dust storms that could last four days would appear on the horizon. Describing a storm that caught her on the way to her barracks, Yoshiko Uchida, author of the book *Desert Exile*, wrote that: "the wind suddenly gathered ominous strength. It swept around us in great thrusting gusts, flinging swirling masses of sand in the air and engulfing us in a thick cloud that eclipsed barracks only ten feet away."

Grit from the dust storms that frequently swept the desert camps seeped into the shoddily built barracks and the belongings of the internees.

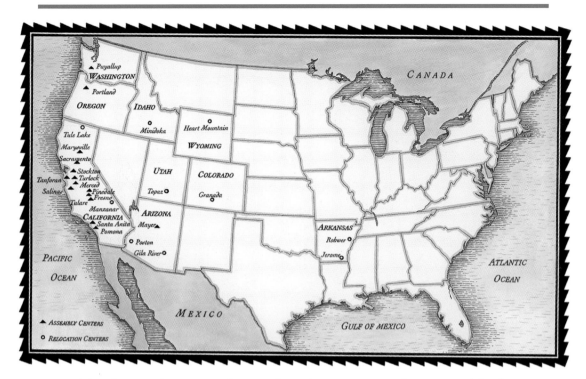

Most of the relocation sites were on the West Coast, but some were as far east—and far from home—as Arkansas.

The Arkansas camps of Jerome and Rohwer, on the other hand, were in swamplands not far from the shores of the Mississippi River and were infested with rattlesnakes and malarial mosquitoes.

All the relocation sites suffered extremes of weather. Manzanar had wind-whipped snow in winter and summer temperatures that reached 115 °F. The camp with the hottest summers was Poston in Arizona, where 120 °F was not uncommon. The coldest winters, −3 °F, were experienced at Heart Mountain in Wyoming.

IN SPITE OF BARE AND INADEQUATE HOUSING, CRUDE WASHING AND TOILET facilities, and the physical hardships of their surroundings, the internees made remarkable progress in bettering their lives. In addition to its

The Japanese made the best of their bare one-room quarters, constructing furniture and putting up hangings, pictures, maps, and seasonal decorations.

administration building, mess halls, and hospital, each camp had a variety of spaces that could be turned into meeting rooms, recreational centers, and especially schoolrooms, because one-quarter of the evacuees were children of school age.

The internees' first efforts, however, went into making their living quarters more homelike. They built shelves, cupboards, and even furniture

Community councils and town hall meetings gave the internees an opportunity to air their problems to administrators.

out of scrap lumber that had been left lying about by the army construction crews. They made window curtains and hangings to subdivide their one-room quarters for privacy. They put up colorful wall posters and calendars. In the absence of fresh flowers they made paper ones to bring a little cheer into their surroundings.

The next step was to organize community councils to set up communications between the internees and the camp administrators. Schools were a priority, starting with the earliest grades and continuing through high school. Teachers were drawn from among the evacuees and also

School-age children, who made up one-fourth of the internee population, were instructed by teachers who were either Japanese internees or Caucasians hired from outside the camps.

from outside the camps. Caucasian teachers provided their services through contracts signed with the WRA. The Japanese teachers were often as good as those from outside the camps. But a Japanese teacher received $16 a month while a Caucasian teacher earned at least $200 a month, plus room and board at the camp.

The same was true for doctors and nurses who staffed the camp hospitals. The maximum salary for a Japanese doctor or nurse was $19 a month, while white staff received the going rate in the outside world, which was $400 to $600 a month.

No one could run a private business in the camps, so the evacuees set up cooperatives to provide goods and services such as extra food items, sewing supplies, household repairs, and beauty parlors. Evacuees who wanted to work in the camp offices, mess halls, laundries, or other facilities could do so for a small monthly salary.

Cooperative stores were set up in the camps to provide everyday needs, including sewing supplies, which were in great demand.

Musical events and other entertainments and pastimes developed by the evacuees helped to lighten spirits.

Others volunteered their time for recreational activities. Poetry, drama, and adult learning groups flourished. Checker and card games were popular with many of the Issei. Still others turned their energies to beautifying the camps with wood sculptures and rock gardens. Young

Young women at Manzanar enjoy a game of softball.

people turned to sports. The evacuees built their own basketball and volleyball courts and baseball diamonds.

Finally, every camp had its own newspaper. Most were published three times a week. Even though the contents had to be cleared with the camp authorities, the Japanese internee editors strove to provide accurate information to their readers. "Truth must be the keystone of this community," wrote the editors of the *Manzanar Free Press* in their first issue on April 11, 1942. Some of the camp newspapers published editions in English and Japanese, and they solicited ads from outside in order to become self-supporting. More importantly, they were a lifeline for an imprisoned people, one in which they could voice their frustrations and try to work out their problems in the company of other internees.

IN THE BOOKLET TITLED *QUESTIONS AND ANSWERS FOR EVACUEES* THAT WAS issued to all newcomers, the government stated that the Japanese had been brought to the relocation camps for their own protection. "Why then," many an internee reflected, "did the guns point inward, toward us, rather than outward, away from us?"

No internee was ever under the illusion that he or she was not a prisoner of war and, even worse, a prisoner who had never been specifically accused of or tried for treasonous activity or any other crime. While families were allowed to live together and the basic needs of food and shelter were supplied, the WRA and its delegates, the immediate camp authorities, had the final word in all matters.

Incoming letters and packages were subjected to careful scrutiny. Items such as cameras and potential weapons such as knives, screwdrivers, and metal files were confiscated. Cakes sent through the mail or delivered by visitors were cut through to make sure they did not conceal any of these things.

Morale in the camps often depended on whether members of the administrative staff were antagonistic to the Japanese. The attitude of the military guards toward the Japanese was even more crucial. Some of the soldiers stationed at the camps were bored and indifferent. But others were openly hostile and trigger-happy. An elderly man at Topaz camp who wandered too close to the barbed-wire fence one day was shot dead. Similar incidents took place in other camps. Even children who were chasing balls or collecting scrap lumber were shot at on occasion.

While most families did not run high physical risks in their new environment, psychological damage affected many. A rift developed between the generations. Issei parents, who had once been respected breadwinners and heads of families, had to give up their authority, not only to their white overseers but to their English-speaking Nisei sons and daughters. The Nisei ran the community councils and were looking ahead to the day when they could leave the camps and realize their ambitions for good jobs and professional careers.

The camp environment also tended to weaken the close-knit nature of Japanese family life. Teenagers in particular clustered in groups and made their way around the camp grounds free of traditional parental restrictions. In the mess halls, young people preferred each others' company at meals to eating with their families.

Kibei youth were often the most disruptive. These young people, who had had an average of five years of schooling in Japan, were viewed by the authorities as potentially the most disloyal. Some Kibei frequently clashed with the JACL because of their contempt for the latter's cooperative approach to the internment.

One twenty-five-year-old Kibei, Harry Ueno, started protests that culminated in an explosion of violence at Manzanar on December 6, 1942. Ueno worked as a cook at the camp and was trying to organize a union for the mess-hall workers. He accused a high-ranking member of the administrative staff of stealing meat and sugar from the Manzanar warehouses.

Widespread rioting resulted when Ueno was arrested on inflated charges of trying to start an uprising and was detained in the county jail. Military police were called in. Hundreds of evacuees, many of them teenagers, were teargassed. Then shots rang out and one young Nisei lay dead. A second victim was mortally wounded and died five days later. Ten other internees were treated for teargassing and for serious gunshot wounds.

The Manzanar riot was not the last of the heated protests to erupt in the camps. Strikes and demonstrations took place throughout the years of internment. They were evidence of the pressures Japanese Americans experienced. The strength and perseverance of the evacuees were remarkable. But it was understandable that patience and standards of conduct would sometimes give way to the frustrations brought on by exile and incarceration.

Most Japanese who had enlisted in the armed forces before Pearl Harbor, like the young soldier seen with his mother, were classified as enemy aliens and discharged after the attack.

Six

Yes-Yes, No-No

BY AUGUST 1942, THE PACIFIC COAST HAD BEEN SUCCESSFULLY CLEARED of all residents of Japanese ancestry. Close to 120,000 individuals had been rounded up, processed through the assembly centers, and reassigned to permanent internment camps where they remained behind barbed wire.

The relocation program had been almost too successful. It was costing the U.S. government millions of dollars to maintain the camps. In addition, the evacuation had withdrawn a very large wartime workforce from the population. Agriculture, the manufacturing sector, and especially defense plants were in need of labor. The armed forces, too, required personnel in ever-increasing numbers.

WRA director Dillon S. Myer tried to find a way to release some of the evacuees from the camps for vital outside work assignments. At the same time, President Franklin Roosevelt came up with a similar approach.

"No loyal citizen of the United States," Roosevelt announced in

RELOCATION CENTER CAPACITIES

Gila River
15,000 persons

Granada
8,000 persons

Heart Mountain
12,000 persons

Jerome
10,000 persons

Manzanar
10,000 persons

Minidoka
10,000 persons

Poston
20,000 persons

Rohwer
10,000 persons

Topaz
10,000 persons

Tule Lake
16,000 persons

1 family = 3,000 persons

Almost 120,000 Japanese residents of the United States were rounded up and placed in internment camps within a year of the government's entry into World War II.

early February 1943, "should be denied the democratic right to exercise the responsibilities of his citizenship, regardless of his ancestry . . . whether it be in the ranks of the armed forces, war production, agriculture, government service, or other work essential to the war effort."

What Roosevelt principally had in mind was the creation of an all-Nisei combat unit to be employed in fighting the war on the European front. The five thousand or so Japanese Americans who had enlisted or been drafted into the armed services under the Selective Service Act of 1940 had for the most part been discharged and classified 4-C [enemy alien] following the attack on Pearl Harbor. Most of those who remained on duty were reassigned to desk, kitchen, or janitorial jobs in stateside units far from the West Coast.

The question that both the WRA and the army felt it needed to explore before civilians or enlisted men could leave the camps was that of loyalty. Ironically, none of the evacuees had been given a chance to avoid internment by swearing their allegiance to the United States. But now that they were incarcerated, the government decided to give them a chance to avow their loyalty to their captors.

Up to this point, one of the groups of internees allowed to leave the camps were some 4,300 college students whose education had been interrupted by the evacuation orders of the spring of 1942. Largely through the efforts of Robert Gordon Sproul, president of the University of California, inland institutions of higher learning were approached regarding the admission of these students.

Sproul wrote to the president of the University of Minnesota: "It is my belief that the efforts that we expend now will be repayed [sic] a thousandfold in the attitude of citizens of Japanese ancestry in years to come."

Not all inland colleges, however, were receptive. Several, including some East Coast schools, refused to admit Nisei students, claiming concern for public reaction and the need for excessive security measures. But a number of state universities, as well as some private and religious schools, agreed to accept them, once permission was granted by the WRA, or the WCCA (if the student was still in an assembly center). President Roosevelt accepted the plan in May 1942.

The government offered students no financial support, so they depended on private subsidies, largely from religious groups. Even at the "welcoming" universities students experienced negative reactions and displays of hostility. Only by not expressing their wounded feelings and by trying to think of themselves as good-will ambassadors to the white community did the young Nisei manage to cling to their educational goals in wartime America.

An even larger number of evacuees released from custody in 1942 were mainly sugar-beet harvesters in Oregon, Utah, and Idaho. Their assignments were temporary and closely monitored, but they earned a little more than the standard camp wages—$15 to $20 a month instead of the $8 to $12 a month paid to nonprofessionals in the camps.

HOW, IN KEEPING WITH PRESIDENT ROOSEVELT'S STATEMENT OF FEBRUARY 1943, was the U.S. government to determine the loyalty of its citizens in order to release them from the camps for purposes of either military service or civilian work clearance?

The answer came in the form of two types of questionnaires, one from the War Department and one from the WRA. The War Department questionnaire was primarily intended to recruit young Nisei for Roosevelt's proposed Japanese combat unit, and was to be answered by males aged seventeen and older. Their reactions to what was in fact a loyalty questionnaire were mixed. Some Nisei who were eager to leave the camps appreciated the invitation to serve but were angered that they would be in a segregated unit just as they were in the relocation centers. Others favored the idea of an all-Nisei unit. They felt that it would give Japanese Americans a chance to prove themselves to the rest of society.

A large proportion wanted no part of the offer to volunteer. They were bitter about their internment and saw no reason to trust or support a government that had violated their constitutional rights. As one young Nisei put it, "Why should I [fight for my country] when the government has taken away our rights and locked us up like a bunch of criminals?"

An especially provocative factor was the unfortunate wording of the loyalty questionnaire. Question 27 simply asked: "Are you willing to serve in the armed forces of the United States on combat duty, wherever ordered?" But Question 28 posed a big problem. It asked Nisei males: "Will you swear unqualified allegiance to the United States of America and faithfully defend the United States from any and all attack by foreign or domestic forces, and forswear any form of allegiance or obedience to the Japanese emperor or any other foreign government, power, or organization?" The WRA civilian version of the loyalty questionnaire presented to Nisei women and Issei of both sexes also asked the internees to "forswear any form of allegiance or obedience to the Japanese emperor."

Among both Nisei and Issei, the question of renouncing loyalty to the emperor provoked a widespread negative reaction. It infuriated Nisei, for if they answered yes it could be assumed that they had been loyal to the emperor all along even though they were American citizens by birth. One Nisei, Togo Tanaka, was so incensed by the suggestion that he and his family might be thought loyal to a foreign power that they "refused to sign the stupid questionnaire" and his family was denied the clearance they had been seeking to leave the camp.

The Issei had a different problem with the question of loyalty to the emperor. By law, they were ineligible for American citizenship and were still technically citizens of Japan. But if they renounced allegiance to Japan they could never return to their homeland and would become stateless individuals, people without a country. Suppose the United States decided to deport them after the war—where would they go? Even if they were allowed to remain U.S. residents, many had relatives in Japan who they hoped to visit after the war. Now they might never see them again. A few even planned to retire to Japan one day.

In order to leave the camps, either for army service or for work opportunities and possible resettlement in a nonmilitary zone, the internees were compelled to answer yes to both Question 27 and Question 28. Answering no to either question marked one as disloyal and ineligible to leave the camps. No to one question was just as bad as no to both.

Soon the entire population became divided into "yes-yes" and "no-no" groups. Families quarreled because some Nisei offspring who wanted to leave said yes to both questions, while their parents said no to both. Within several weeks, Question 28 was reworded to omit any references to the emperor of Japan. But by then most of the applications had been filled out and the entire registration process was nearing completion.

One older Nisei expressed his anger this way:

I said "no" and I'm going to stick to "no". . . . If this country doesn't want me they can throw me out. What do they know about loyalty? I'm as loyal as anyone in this country. . . . What business did they have asking me a question like that?

I was born in Hawaii. I worked most of my life on the west coast. I have never been to Japan. . . . My wife and I lost $10,000 in that evacuation. She had a beauty parlor and had to give that up. I had a good position worked up as a gardener, and was taken away from that. We had a little home and that's gone now. . . .

That's not the American way, taking everything away from people. . . . Where are the Germans? Where are the Italians? Do they ask them questions about loyalty?

THE RECRUITMENT DRIVE IN THE TEN RELOCATION CENTERS RESULTED IN a total of only 1,181 Nisei volunteering for military service. The government had hoped for 3,000. A similar drive for volunteers had been launched in Hawaii, where there were no detention camps and where no loyalty tests had been administered. There, nearly 10,000 Nisei volunteered for combat, and the government quota had called for only 1,500.

Fair play and respect for the Japanese segment of the population in Hawaii had made the difference. The importance of treating a besieged people with understanding, even in the camps on the mainland, was demonstrated by the directors of Minidoka in Idaho. Five days before the army recruiters arrived, the inappropriately worded questionnaire was

Japanese volunteers recruited for military service in 1943 were relatively few in number because of the controversial loyalty oath.

Mothers whose sons went into the army remained in the internment camps where they were presented with service flags.

discussed in public forums. Grievances were aired, and troublesome issues were addressed. As a result, Minidoka contributed the largest number of volunteers.

Tule Lake camp in northern California, on the other hand, contributed the smallest number, due to the camp authorities' refusal to discuss the questionnaire with internees. In addition, internees were told that filling out the War Department loyalty questionnaires was compulsory, and that those who resisted would be punished under the Espionage Act, both of which were untrue.

Tule Lake's troubles became evident on the night of February 21,

1943, when a group of thirty-five seventeen- and eighteen-year-old Nisei banded together in protest. Terror and intimidation followed as troops were called in, the young men were torn from their families' arms, herded into waiting trucks, and carted off to the county jail.

When they learned that the young men had not violated the Selective Service Act and were not liable for the $10,000 fine and twenty-year jail sentence threatened by the camp authorities, the internees expressed more outrage. Although the youths were released from custody, Tule Lake's problems were just beginning.

Of the 75,000 adults throughout the ten relocation centers who were required to answer the questionnaires, about 9,000 had answered no-no or had left the forms blank. There were many different reasons that had nothing to do with disloyalty. Some answered no out of peer group loyalty, fear of family separation, sheer confusion, and especially bitterness regarding the injustice of their incarceration.

"What do they take us for?" a Nisei named Dunks Oshima wanted to know. "First they change my army status to 4-C because of my ancestry, run me out of town, and now they want me to volunteer . . . so I could get killed for this . . . democracy."

Now, however, that the "disloyal" had supposedly been identified, the WRA sought a way of physically separating them from the "loyal" internees. Since Tule Lake had already registered the largest number of negative responses to the questionnaire (42 percent), it was chosen to become a maximum-security segregation center. It was to be guarded by an extra one thousand military personnel and flanked by six army tanks, set to go in the event of insurrection.

By the fall of 1943, 6,000 "loyal" internees were moved out of Tule Lake and sent to other camps to make room for 12,000 "disloyals" plus family members who did not want to be separated from them. Soon 16,000 prisoners were crowded into the one-story barracks of Tule Lake. Conditions were so harsh that Judge William Denman of the Ninth

"Disloyal" internees were moved to the Tule Lake Relocation Center (shown here after a thaw), which became notorious for its harsh conditions and gang violence.

Circuit Court of Appeals wrote after the war, on August 26, 1949: "No federal penitentiary so treats its adult prisoners. Here were the children and babies as well. . . . To reach the unheated latrines, which were in the center of the blocks of fourteen buildings, meant leaving the residential shacks and walking through the rain and snow. . . . In the cells of a federal penitentiary there is no such crowding."

An even more severe situation at Tule Lake was the presence of an extremely militant Japanese-American faction made up mainly of Kibei. So fierce was their opposition to the incarceration and to the loyalty questionnaire that many had declared their intention to renounce their U.S. citizenship and to return to Japan to live after the war.

This ultranationalist group set up schools at Tule Lake to teach Japanese language and customs to prepare for their repatriation. They also performed Japanese calisthenics and military exercises on the camp

Japanese ultranationalists board a vessel for repatriation to Japan; some 8,000 left at their own request after the war.

grounds and soon became known as the "pressure boys" because they used intimidation and strong-arm tactics even on their fellow detainees, most of whom were bitter and disillusioned but had no intention of turning pro-Japanese.

The high concentration of extremists and belligerents in one prison camp was bound to lead to violence. Gang fights, work stoppages, food fights, and open rebellion against the administrators became commonplace. By November 1943, martial law, or rule by the military, was declared at Tule Lake. Tanks entered the camp, machine guns were mounted at strategic positions, and several hundred internees were locked up in the camp stockade, a prison within a prison where beatings and other abuses were said to have been inflicted. Even when martial law ended two months later, incidents of violence continued to plague Tule Lake.

Nisei infantrymen of the 442d distinguished themselves in France in October 1944, suffering heavy losses in their rescue of the "Lost Battalion."

Seven

The Road Back

THE YEAR 1944 BROUGHT SIGNIFICANT CHANGES IN THE DIRECTION OF the war and, by its close, victory for the United States and its allies appeared to be in sight. For the Japanese-American internees, however, there was still a troubling and painful road ahead.

Despite the poor results of the loyalty questionnaire in recruiting a Nisei combat force from the relocation camps, the government went ahead with its military plans. In March 1943, the army assembled an all-Japanese fighting force made up of fewer than 1,200 volunteers from the camps, volunteers from Hawaii and outside the camps, and Nisei who had joined the army before Pearl Harbor but had been kept from active duty. This fighting unit became known as the 442d Regimental Combat Team. Another all-Japanese outfit, the 100th Infantry Battalion, originating in the Hawaiian National Guard, had been activated nine months earlier, in June 1942.

Both units were sent to Mississippi for intensive training. The Hawaiian 100th was ready for combat by September 1943 and it was shipped to North Africa for the fierce fighting that accomplished an Allied invasion of Italy.

Although numerous Nisei from Hawaii had volunteered for the 100th Battalion and the 442d, they both needed to be reinforced for the battles that lay ahead. On January 14, 1944, the secretary of war announced the reinstatement of the draft for Nisei living in the camps, as well as any who had not been interned because they were not Pacific Coast residents.

The JACL had long urged such a step as a means of proving Japanese Americans' patriotism, and the WRA favored it as a means of reducing the population of the camps. This time, the major voices of rebellion came from the Heart Mountain Relocation Center in Wyoming. A group that called itself the Fair Play Committee and that was deeply opposed to the JACL position argued against the mandatory army induction of citizens whose constitutional rights had been violated. Why should Japanese Americans be forced to fight for "liberty and justice for all" when it had been denied them?

By 1944, however, the Nisei in the relocation centers were ready to respond more positively to the draft than they had to the request for volunteers a year earlier. Entering military service was one way to relieve the tedium of life in the camps, speed the progress of the war, and perhaps to prepare for better opportunities in the postwar era. The resistance to induction counseled by the Heart Mountain Fair Play Committee had almost no success. Sixty-three draft-eligible Nisei at Heart Mountain who had refused to report for induction were tried. They were convicted and, in June 1944, they were sentenced to three years in federal prison.

Meanwhile, the ranks of the 442d were growing. By the spring of 1944, it was already becoming an elite unit due to the high educational qualifications of many of its inductees. At the same time, women internees were signing up in increasing numbers for the Women's Army Corps (WAC) and the Army Nurse Corps.

The accomplishments of the 442d Regimental Combat Team were exceptional. The unit realized its motto, "Go for Broke," in one daring undertaking after another. After joining the Hawaiian 100th Infantry Battalion in the bloody fighting in Italy, the 442d went on to France. Its rescue of the "Lost Battalion," a Texas unit trapped behind German enemy lines in the French countryside, resulted in a 60 percent casualty rate. For its final campaign, the 442d returned to Italy, where it took part in the push to drive the Germans out completely.

Fighting with the 442d in northern Italy in April 1945 was Lieutenant Daniel Inouye. He lost an arm in the attack. After Hawaii became a state in 1949, Inouye was the first American of Japanese ancestry to serve in the U.S. House of Representatives. In 1962, he was elected to the U.S. Senate to serve for many terms.

Nisei were also active in the Pacific theater of war, principally as interpreters and decoders. While only 10 percent of American-born Japanese who had been schooled on the mainland knew the Japanese language, the Kibei were fluent in it, and their work proved highly valuable.

Kenny Yasui demonstrated that the suspicions leveled at the Kibei were very often groundless. While on duty on the India-Burma front, Yasui encountered the enemy. He posed as a Japanese colonel, and captured sixteen Japanese soldiers by giving commands in Japanese, which he had learned as a student in Tokyo.

A total of 33,000 Japanese Americans, a little more than half from the mainland and the rest from Hawaii, served in World War II. The 442d Regimental Combat Team was one of the most decorated in history. It suffered 9,486 dead and wounded, and received more than 18,000 individual decorations. These included one Congressional Medal of Honor, 52 Distinguished Service Crosses, 560 Silver Stars, 810 Bronze Stars, and more than 3,600 Purple Hearts.

Daniel Inouye, who fought with the 442d in Italy in April 1945, became the first Japanese American to serve in both houses of Congress.

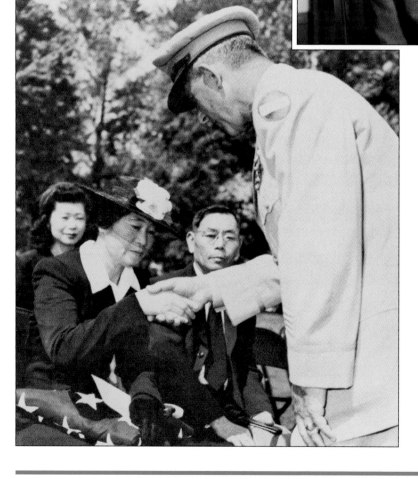

The mother of the first Nisei to be buried in Arlington National Cemetery is presented with a flag by World War II General Jacob L. Devers.

Yet when newly promoted Captain Daniel Inouye entered a barber-shop near San Francisco for a haircut on his way home to Hawaii, the barber questioned him about his ancestry. Was he perhaps . . . Chinese?

Inouye, in his medal-emblazoned uniform, with a hook where his right hand was supposed to be, replied, "I am an American."

"Don't give me that American stuff," the barber shot back. "You're a Jap and we don't cut Jap hair."

WHILE THE NISEI SOLDIERS WERE FIGHTING ABROAD, THEIR FAMILIES back home were gradually being released from the camps, not only for work furloughs but for resettlement in various parts of the U.S. away from the West Coast. The general ban on returning to California, Oregon, and Washington was not lifted until January 1945.

In June 1944, President Franklin Roosevelt began to give some thought as to how the released Japanese internees could be reintegrated into American life. Already, Jerome camp in Arkansas was about to close and the WRA hoped to resettle as many as possible of its remaining internees rather than have to transfer them to other camps.

The president was treading carefully regarding resettlement because he planned to run for an unprecedented fourth term in November and he was seeking "internal quiet." He did not want racial issues to flare up and possibly cost him votes. Roosevelt agreed with political leaders on the West Coast that even if the Japanese were eventually allowed to return to their former communities, such a move must be "nothing sudden and not in too great quantities at any one time."

A preferable solution, Roosevelt felt, would be to distribute "one or two families to each county as a start [in] the Middle West, the East, and the South" as "a great method of avoiding a public outcry."

As a result, many of those who had responded yes-yes to the loyalty questionnaires and who had special job skills were resettled in 1944 in parts of the country that were entirely new to them. Stenographers and

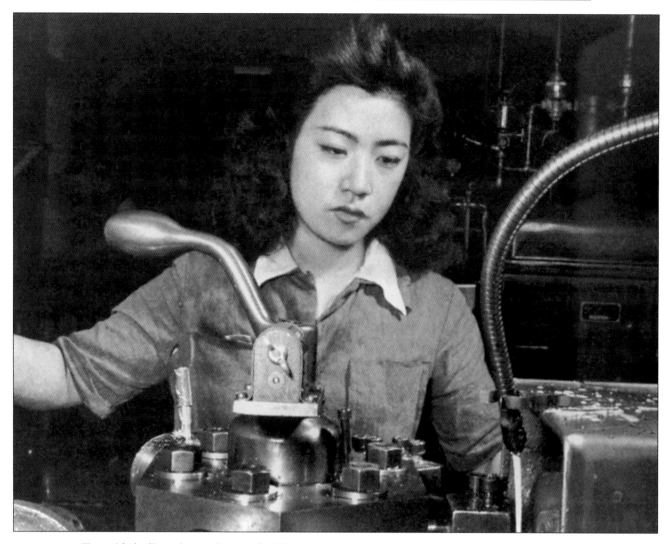

To avoid the lingering racism on the West Coast, many Japanese Americans, like the Chicago defense-plant worker above, left the camps to work in the Midwest or the East.

typists relocated to New England for civil service and defense-related jobs. Chicago and other midwestern cities became home to those who had technical skills and to those who opted for defense plant work.

Theresa Takayoshi, a young mother who had been an internee at Minidoka camp, told how fortunate she felt when her husband was offered a job as an accountant in Indianapolis. "I think the biggest help was not coming back to Seattle right away. During the twenty-five years we spent in Indiana we met many, many nice people. They were all Caucasians and they all accepted us as if we were just one of them. And not one of them knew about the evacuation, not one. When I would tell them about it, they were aghast."

For others who also had no choice but to relocate to an unfamiliar area, the bitterness of their wartime experience never went away. Chiye Tomihiro's father, an Issei, was a legal advisor serving the Japanese community in Portland, Oregon, before the evacuation. He had to resettle in Chicago when he came out of internment. Tomohiro wrote, "he didn't have any money. No capital. No nothing, and even with his education . . . a sixty-year-old man trying to get a white collar job—there was nothing available for him. . . . Finally he decided he would try opening some kind of office and do bookkeeping services and try to sell real estate and things like that. He never was able to get back on his feet in the real sense of the word. I think that after having gone through the whole trauma of the Depression, and then, just when he was getting back on his feet, to have this second setback. I think that was just too much."

Even after the government's announcement in December 1944 that all camps would close by the end of 1945 and that the evacuees could return to the West Coast, there were those who appeared fearful of leaving the camps. The Issei in particular, many of whom were elderly and demoralized, tended to want to huddle together in the relocation centers. During the years of incarceration they had lost their authority as heads of families. They had also lost homes, farms, and businesses that had taken almost a lifetime of hard work to acquire. There seemed to be nothing to go back to. Nor did the WRA offer any sort of economic assistance to help the Issei and other displaced internees to resettle and rebuild their lives. The 35,000 or so evacuees who still lingered in the camps by the time the war with Japan ended in August 1945 were given $25 each ($50

A group of internees at Manzanar wait to board the buses that will take them back to their former homes on the Pacific Coast.

for families) and train fare back to the point of evacuation. There was no compensation for their financial losses and mental suffering. They were on their own.

ALTHOUGH FRANKLIN ROOSEVELT HAD BEEN RE-ELECTED IN NOVEMBER 1944, he continued to caution the former internees to scatter themselves "all around the United States," so as not to "discombobulate" the existing communities in American society. Yet, once it became possible to return to the Pacific Coast farmlands, towns, and cities where they had formerly lived, the desire of the evacuees to go home was uppermost.

What did those who had spent years of incarceration in the isolated camps find on returning to their former communities? Some were welcomed by special committees that supplied them with hot food and overnight lodging as they stepped off the trains in Los Angeles, San Francisco, and Seattle. But more were greeted with the same hostile signs as before at town limits and in store windows: NO JAPS ALLOWED. NO JAPS SERVED.

Rural districts were the most dangerous for returning evacuee families. Night riders roamed the countryside setting fires or sending rifle shots into reoccupied dwellings on the farms and ranches. Death threats were delivered via notes and telephone calls.

A great many returnees found their homes in complete disrepair and their fields in ruins. New housing was almost nonexistent. None had been built due to wartime priorities. At the same time, more than a million Americans had moved to California from the Midwest and the South during the war years. As a result, the released internees had to move into trailer camps, rooming houses, Quonset huts, and other temporary shelters. Some became live-in servants so that they would have a roof over their heads.

In many respects, those who had sold their property, even at a steep loss, were better off than those who had asked others to care for it. During their absence, homes and farms were lost for nonpayment of mortgages or taxes. Vandalism also took a heavy toll. Some evacuees had stored their personal belongings or their business inventories in Buddhist temples that had subsequently been broken into and their contents destroyed.

Ironically, aggression against the returnees continued during the very time that the 442d Regimental Combat Team was suffering its heaviest

Hostile signs on building entrances and storefronts greeted the Japanese Americans when they returned from the camps.

losses on the European front. General Joseph Stillwell, a hero of the war in the Pacific, praised the Nisei fighting men of World War II. He said that they had "brought an awful big hunk of America with their blood" and added, "We cannot allow a single injustice to the Nisei without defeating the purposes for which we fought."

Yet when the parents of Shig Doi, a soldier in the 442d, were released from the Granada camp (also known as Amache) in Colorado and returned to their orchard in Placer County, California, Shig said "they hit a brick wall."

Since the land on which Shig's family had grown peaches, pears, and grapes was free of mortgage debt, they had been able to lease the property during their absence and then reclaim it. However, the first thing that happened, Shig reported, was, "they [racist vigilantes] were going to dynamite our packing shed, but somehow the fuse didn't go off. So second, they were going to burn it down."

Fortunately, somebody warned Shig's brother and he doused the flames with a fire hose. "Then the following night they fired a shotgun through our house. When I got home my mother showed me where all these pellet marks were. . . . See, I was getting shot at from the enemy, and then at home in my own country, people were shooting at my dad. I was risking my life for this country, and my government was not protecting my folks."

SLOWLY, VERY SLOWLY, THE ANTI-JAPANESE ATTACKS, THREATS, AND RHETOric began to die down. The American Legion, adamantly pro-internment during the war years, had no choice but to acknowledge the fine record and extraordinary sacrifices of the 442d Regimental Combat Team. Fletcher Bowron, the mayor of Los Angeles and originally a strong supporter of evacuation, proclaimed on the steps of city hall in January 1945 that he wanted all those "of Japanese ancestry who have relocated here to feel secure in your home." Eugene V. Rostow, the Yale law professor who in 1955 became dean of the Yale Law School, stated: "One hundred thousand persons were sent to concentration camps on a record which wouldn't support a conviction for stealing a dog."

Public apologies and statements of regret went part of the way toward calming the West Coast communities to which the former Japanese-American residents returned. But was there to be no compensation for the physical and mental suffering and the personal injuries and deaths that had taken place in the camps, the income the internees might have earned during the war years had they been free, and the property they had been forced to sell, leave in the hands of others, or simply abandon?

Starting with the first announcements of the camp closings, the JACL had begun lobbying Congress for a way to compensate the former internees for property losses. Accordingly, the Evacuation Claims Act,

In 1946, even as President Harry S. Truman was bestowing honors on the 442d, racist vigilantes were harassing the families of Nisei who had served in the war.

which was finally signed into law by President Harry Truman in 1948, provided for "tangible" losses only, such as homes and businesses that had been neglected by tenants, vandalized, or destroyed. Their value was to be based on the original price or, if provable, their 1942 value.

Possessions of sentimental worth such as old photographs or carefully cultivated bonsai plants that might have been sold for thousands of dollars were not eligible for claim. Nor were the broken and toppled gravestones in Japanese-American cemeteries or the monies deposited in bank accounts that had been frozen upon evacuation. Above all, the funds distributed under the Evacuation Claims Act were not meant to represent any sort of admission of wrongdoing on the part of the United States government.

The claims process under the 1948 act went on for seventeen years and was fraught with litigation for which the claimants were forced to pay uncompensated legal fees. When the last claim was settled, in 1965, the tally was as follows: The total of the property lost by the internees was $400 million, for which they received less than ten cents on the dollar. The government paid out not quite $37 million and added no interest for the length of time so many of the claimants had had to wait for remuneration.

The only wholly positive development of the early postwar years was the passage of the McCarran-Walter Act in 1952, abolishing racial qualifications for citizenship. The Issei could now be naturalized. By 1965, 46,000 Issei had become American citizens.

During the long wait for redress of the wrongs inflicted by Japanese internment, the Nisei population began to age; a veteran attends an anniversary service at the cemetery at Pearl Harbor.

Eight

After a Long Silence

IN THE YEARS IMMEDIATELY FOLLOWING THE RELEASE OF THE JAPANESE Americans, legal scholars, military figures, and even local officials came forward with statements of remorse. But would the United States government ever apologize for the constitutional violations it inflicted?

More than thirty years passed following the signing of Executive Order 9066 before the long silence was broken. The impetus came from the JACL, which began in 1976 to put forth a plan for some official form of restitution for the internees that would serve as a long-overdue admission of the wrong that had been done them.

With demands for redress becoming increasingly urgent, the government's first response was the official revocation of Executive Order 9066. On February 19, 1976, the thirty-fourth anniversary of the signing of President Roosevelt's evacuation order, President Gerald Ford admitted that internment was among our "national mistakes." He stated:

"not only was the evacuation wrong, but Japanese Americans were and are loyal Americans."

The JACL, however, continued to press for the distribution of individual reparation payments. At its Salt Lake City convention in 1978, it proposed that every surviving evacuee should receive a symbolic sum of $25,000.

The JACL proposal led to the formation of the Congressional Commission on Wartime Relocation and Internment of Civilians (CWRIC) whose purpose was to conduct hearings, examine documents, interview internees and officials about the relocation, decide the extent of the wrong committed, and determine what would constitute an appropriate remedy.

The process took two and a half years. In February 1983, after examining more than 10,000 documents and taking testimony from at least 750 witnesses, the CWRIC issued its report, *Personal Justice Denied*. The report concluded that the evacuation and internment of 120,000 Japanese Americans was "not justified by military necessity." It further stated: "A grave injustice was done to American citizens and resident aliens who . . . were excluded, removed, and detained by the United States during World War II . . . based on race prejudice, war hysteria, and a failure of political leadership."

The commission recommended that each surviving evacuee receive a sum of $20,000 as restitution. As no sum of money could possibly compensate for the broken lives of so many of the survivors or for the dead who could recoup nothing, it had to be viewed only as a symbolic gesture.

More time was to pass, and more survivors were to die off, before the Civil Liberties Act of 1988 was passed. It authorized the $20,000 reparations payments to each of the estimated 60,000 surviving internees, starting with the eldest. President Ronald Reagan signed the bill into law on August 10, 1988. A 1992 amendment appropriated additional funds because the actual number of survivors turned out to be 80,000.

The actual distribution of the monies, however, did not begin until October 1990. By this time, George H. W. Bush was president. In an official letter accompanying each check, President Bush wrote: "A monetary sum and words alone cannot restore lost years or erase painful memories. . . . We can never fully right the wrongs of the past. But . . . in enacting a law calling for restitution and offering a sincere apology, your fellow Americans have . . . renewed their traditional commitment to the ideals of freedom, equality, and justice."

On October 9, 1990, the oldest survivor of the internment received his check and a letter of apology, which were presented to him in person. He was Mamoru Eto, wheelchair-bound and 107 years old.

TODAY THE CAMPS ARE EMPTY; MOST HAVE CEASED TO EXIST IN THEIR original form. Their frail barracks and gatehouses, victim to desert winds and dust storms, blizzards or intense heat, were long ago reduced to bleached wood and ragged tar paper. But at one camp, Manzanar, which was established as a National Historic Site in 1992, the barbed-wire fence has been restored, the gatehouses and sentry posts have been rehabilitated, and the cemetery enclosure made of black locust tree branches has been rebuilt.

So that none will forget the Manzanar camp of the war years, one of its eight guard towers and two of its barracks are to be reconstructed. To more fully commemorate the internment, the auditorium will be converted to a visitors center where photographs and documents can be displayed.

As the best-preserved of the former camp sites, Manzanar has been host to an annual spring pilgrimage of Japanese Americans and other visitors since 1969. Nisei, as well as Sansei and Yonsei—second- and third-generation American-born Japanese—come to Manzanar to visit the crumbling gravestones in the desert and to pay homage to the family memories that have been shared with them.

In the minds of all those who visit Manzanar there must always be

Manzanar, which has become a national historic site, is now visited regularly by young Japanese Americans and their families; the visitors are seated at the base of the camp's cemetery monument.

the question of whether such a sweeping violation of human rights could ever take place in the United States again. Each time a specific group of American citizens or resident aliens is targeted by the self-righteous and the superpatriotic, there is reason to be concerned that it might. Ethnic and racial prejudice, economic greed, and political self-seeking have not disappeared from American life. *Liberty, equality, and justice for all* must continue to be the watchwords of a proud nation.

Notes

p. 11, Ito, Kazuo. Issei: *A History of Japanese Immigration in North America.* Seattle: Japanese Community Service, 1973.

p. 17, Sato, Yuriko. "Emigration of Issei Women." Asian American Studies, University of California, Berkeley, 1982.

p. 21, Kikumura, Akemi. *Through Harsh Winters: The Life of a Japanese Immigrant Woman.* Novato, CA: Chandler and Sharp, 1981.

p. 24, Ito.

p. 30, Mears, Eliot. *Resident Orientals on the American Pacific Coast.* New York: Ayer Co., 1927.

p. 35, quoted in Tateishi, John, ed. *And Justice for All: An Oral History of the Japanese American Detention Camps.* New York: Random House, 1984.

pp. 35–36, Ibid.

p. 39, Ibid.

p. 39, Ibid.

p. 50, Journal of Mr. H, quoted in Bosworth, Allan R. *America's Concentration Camps.* W. W. Norton, Co., 1967.

p. 52, Ibid.

p. 52, Minoru Yasui, quoted in Tateishi, *And Justice for All.*

pp.54–55, Letter to Grace Nichold, June 1942: Conrad-Devenek Collection, Hoover Institution Archives.

p. 61, quoted in Tateishi, *And Justice for All.*

p. 62, Letter from Milton Eisenhower to Agriculture Secretary Claude Wickard, April 1, 1942; correspondence of the secretary of agriculture, foreign relations, 2-1, Aliens-Refugees Record Group 16, National Archives

pp. 63–64, quoted in Personal Justice Denied.

pp. 77–78, President Franklin D. Roosevelt's files, University of California Archives, Bancroft Library.

p. 80, quoted in *Personal Justice Denied.*

pp. 81–82, Togo Tanaka, quoted in Davis, Daniel S. *Behind Barbed Wire: The Imprisonment of Japanese Americans during World War II.* New York: Dutton, 1982.

p. 85, quoted in Sone, Monica. *Nisei Daughter.* Boston: Little Brown, 1973.

p. 93, Inouye, Daniel K., with Lawrence Elliott. *Journey to Washington.* Englewood Cliffs, NJ: Prentice-Hall, 1967.

p. 95, Chihe Tomihiro, quoted in Tateishi, *And Justice for All.*

p. 97, President Franklin D. Roosevelt press conference 982, November 21, 1944, FDR Library, Hyde Park, NY.

p. 98, Shig Doi, quoted in Tateishi, *And Justice for All.*

Bibliography

Adams, Ansel, John Hershey, John Armor, and Peter Wright. *Manzanar*. New York: Times Books, 1988.

Bosworth, Allan R. *America's Concentration Camps*. New York: W. W. Norton, 1967.

Cao, Lan, and Himilce Novas. *Everything You Need to Know about Asian-American History*. New York: Penguin, 1996.

Daniels, Roger. *Concentration Camps U.S.A.: Japanese Americans and World War II*. New York: Holt, Rinehart and Winston, 1972.

Daniels, Roger. *Prisoners Without Trial: Japanese Americans in World War II*. New York: Hill and Wang, 1993.

Embrey, Sue Kunitomi, ed. *The Lost Years: 1942–1946*. Los Angeles: Moonlight Publications, 1972.

Inouye, Daniel K., with Lawrence Elliott. *Journey to Washington*. Englewood Cliffs, NJ: Prentice-Hall, 1967.

Kessler, Lauren. *Stubborn Twig: Three Generations in the Life of a Japanese Family*. New York: Random House, 1993.

Morton, W. Scott. *Japan: Its History and Culture*. New York: McGraw-Hill, 1994.

O'Brien, David J., and Stephen S. Fugita. *The Japanese American Experience*. Bloomington and Indianapolis, IN: Indiana University Press, 1991.

Report of the Commission on Wartime Relocation and Internment of Civilians. *Personal Justice Denied*. Washington, D.C.: U.S. Government Printing Office, 1992.

Takaki, Ronald. *Strangers from a Different Shore: A History of Asian Americans*. Boston: Little Brown, 1998.

Takezawa, Yasuko I. *Breaking the Silence: Redress and Japanese American Ethnicity*. Ithaca, NY: Cornell University Press, 1995.

Tateishi, John, ed. *And Justice for All: An Oral History of the Japanese American Detention Camps*. New York: Random House, 1984.

Weglyn, Michi. *Years of Infamy: The Untold Story of America's Concentration Camps*. Seattle, WA: University of Washington Press, 1996.

Further Reading

Brimner, Larry Dane. *Voices from the Camps: Internment of Japanese Americans during World War II*. New York: Franklin Watts, 1994.

Davis, Daniel S. *Behind Barbed Wire: The Imprisonment of Japanese Americans during World War II*. New York: Dutton, 1982.

Houston, Jeanne Wakatsuki, and James D. Houston. *Farewell to Manzanar*. Boston: Houghton Mifflin, 1973.

Stefoff, Rebecca and Ronald Takaki. *Spacious Dreams: The First Wave of Asian Immigration*. New York: Chelsea House, 1994.

Tunnell, Michael O., and George W. Chilcoat. *The Children of Topaz: The Story of a Japanese-American Internment Camp Based on a Classroom Diary*. New York: Holiday House, 1996.

Uchida, Yoshiko. *Desert Exile: The Uprooting of a Japanese American Family*. Seattle, WA: University of Washington Press, 1982.

Yancey, Diane. *Life in a Japanese American Internment Camp*. San Diego, CA: Lucent Books, 1998.

Index

Page numbers for illustrations are in **boldface**.